BLAKE
and the Assimilation
of Chaos

BLAKE
and the Assimilation of Chaos

Christine Gallant

PRINCETON UNIVERSITY PRESS
PRINCETON, NEW JERSEY

1978

Library of Congress Cataloging in Publication Data will be
found on the last printed page of this book

Publication of this book has been aided by a grant from the
Paul Mellon Fund of Princeton University Press

This book has been composed in V.I.P. Garamond

Clothbound editions of Princeton University Press books are
printed on acid-free paper, and binding materials
are chosen for strength and durability

Printed in the United States of America by Princeton
University Press, Princeton, New Jersey

Listen,
I will tell thee
what is done in moments
to thee unknown.

JERUSALEM 1.7.29

Acknowledgments

I would like to thank here those who have helped me along the way as I wrote this book:

James Scoggins, Professor of English at Virginia Polytechnic Institute and State University, whose open-minded encouragement of a critical approach not at all his own kept me writing in the early days;

David Erdman, equally and generously tolerant, whose perceptive questions led me to see that Blake explored social as well as psychological Chaos;

and my husband James, also a writer, with whom I enjoyed so many battles about language and style. Furthermore, he did the dishes.

Contents

Acknowledgments
vii

Abbreviations
xi

Introduction
3

ONE. Myth and Non-Myth
9

TWO. The Balance of Archetypes in *The Four Zoas*
48

THREE. The Reassumption of Ancient Bliss
95

FOUR. Going Forth to the Vintage of Nations
116

FIVE. Beyond Myth, Beyond Non-Myth
155

Bibliography
187

Index
197

Abbreviations

A	*America: A Prophecy*
Aion	*Aion: Researches into the Phenomenology of the Self,* 2nd edition
Archetypes	*Archetypes and the Collective Unconscious,* 2nd edition
BA	*The Book of Ahania*
BL	*The Book of Los*
BU	*The Book of Urizen*
E	*Europe: A Prophecy*
FZ	*The Four Zoas*
GA	*The Ghost of Abel*
J	*Jerusalem*
MHH	*The Marriage of Heaven and Hell*
M	*Milton*
P & P	*The Poetry and Prose of William Blake,* 2nd edition
SL	*The Song of Los*
S. of E.	*Songs of Experience*
S. of I.	*Songs of Innocence*
Structure	*The Structure and Dynamics of the Psyche,* 2nd edition
Two Essays	*Two Essays on Analytical Psychology,* 2nd edition

BLAKE
and the Assimilation
of Chaos

Introduction

THERE are important areas of Blake's work that I will be considering here only in passing or not at all: namely, his radical and political side, his philosophical thinking, and his art. Certainly, Blake's poetry lies in the mainstream of British radicalism of his time; his thought is as rigorous, original, and consistent as that of any philosopher of his time (or, some would argue, any since); and his poetry is largely entwined inextricably with the artwork surrounding it on the engraved plates of the poems or the manuscript pages of *The Four Zoas*. Yet Blake criticism has now reached a point where the foundation of understanding has been laid, and these important areas have been excellently covered by earlier scholar-critics. What interests me is not so much the outlines of Blake's mythic "system," or its encyclopedic nature, which managed to include most of what was happening around him, but rather the *function* that the very process of mythmaking had for him. Blake himself seems to have been consciously preoccupied with this same question, in ways I hope to show in the rest of this book.

What I am attempting in this study is a psychological reading of Blake's poetry that is Jungian in orientation, yet still grants the work of art its own stubborn autonomy. Jungian psychology seems particularly apt for understanding this Romantic poet, since Jung himself in many ways is neo-Romantic (perhaps because, like Freud, he was raised near the end of the Romantic period in Europe), and many of the ideas now considered most characteristically Romantic structure his thought. Yet there are well-publicized pitfalls in psychological approaches to literature that I find alluring enough, but hope to avoid. It is suspiciously easy to translate Blake's myth and poetry into a Jungian framework; suspicious because Blake is left behind, subsumed into Jung's own "system." *The Four*

Zoas is especially vulnerable to such treatment, since it is easy to equate the four Zoas with the four Jungian personality "functions" of Intuition, Feeling, Sensation, and Thinking. Blake's "Regeneration" becomes Jungian "Individuation"; the Emanations become animae because they are female and reside in the male psyche (except for Shiloh, the masculine Emanation of France); Albion's "Sleep" and subsequent awakening in the apocalypse become ego differentiation from the collective unconscious; and (ultimate degradation of the poet's being) Blake becomes Jung's "intuitive introvert" because he claimed to have seen visions and roundly asserted, "I question not my Corporeal or Vegetative Eye any more than I would Question a Window concerning a Sight I look thro & not with it."[1]

But whatever the dangers, I think that Jungian psychology may still prove valuable in the analysis of this poem and Blake's poetry in general. *The Four Zoas* is above all a study in man's psychology, and it seems entirely appropriate to use modern depth psychology in an attempt to understand this poem, which purports to take place "in the Human Brain" (*FZ* 1.11.16). Indeed, I will argue that it is *only* through attention to the changing pattern of Jungian archetypes in the poem during its ten-year period of composition that one can see the profound change occurring in Blake's myth as it expanded from a closed, static system to a dynamic, ongoing process.

Therefore, it seems necessary to set forth those elements of Jungian psychology that will form the interpretative cornerstone for my study of the change from the myth of the "Lambeth" prophecies to that of the major prophecies. I do not mean to seem patronizing, and much of this will be quite familiar to some of my readers. But many of the critics who discuss the workings of the unconscious in literature do not seem to realize that they are using the Freudian definition of the unconscious, a definition not held by all depth psycholo-

---

[1] *The Poetry and Prose of William Blake,* 2nd edition, p. 555. All quotations from Blake's poetry and prose are taken from this edition, hereafter cited as *P & P.* For examples of psychoanalysis of Blake the man, see June Singer, *The Unholy Bible*; and W. P. Witcutt, *Blake, A Psychological Study.*

gists. Also, I think it important to note that "archetypal" criticism does not use the word "archetype" in a Jungian sense at all, whatever its adherents may claim, for Jungian archetypes are not passive semimythological motifs or recurring literary genres.

Jung sees the psyche as being divided into consciousness (which he terms the ego) and the unconscious. Consciousness is what is known of oneself by oneself, all that is rational and comprehensible to the understanding. This ego is frequently influenced by the unconscious, whose structure is fairly chaotic and unsystematic, unlike the logical structure of consciousness. The difference between Freud's and Jung's conceptions of the unconscious is one of the most basic differences between them, for the unconscious as Jung sees it is much more than that psychic area into which painful and destructive thoughts and memories have been repressed. There certainly is this layer to the unconscious, and Jung calls it the "personal" unconscious. But he holds that there is a second layer underlying this first, which he terms the "collective" unconscious. "I call it 'collective,' " he writes, "because, unlike the personal unconscious, it is not made up of individual . . . contents but of those which are universal and of regular occurrence."[2] And elsewhere he writes that the collective unconscious "forms . . . an omnipresent, unchanging . . . *quality . . . of the psyche per se.*"[3] The unconscious as a whole is the world of intuition, instincts, and the emotions, a self-contained world having its own reality, just as the outer world has *its* reality.[4] It constantly tries to complement consciousness by reconciling rationality with instinctual emotions, and a recognition of the unconscious and its powerful influence upon the ego is necessary for any unification of the Self. (It is important not to confuse Jung's Self with Blake's Selfhood, for by his term Jung means all parts of the personality: the ego, the personal unconscious, and the collective unconscious.)

From the collective unconscious come the archetypes, asso-

[2] Jung, *Structure*, p. 134.   [3] Jung, *Aion*, p. 7.
[4] Jung, *Two Essays*, p. 185.

ciated closely with the instincts. It should be noted that Jung says that it is the *predisposition* to certain "constantly repeated experiences of humanity"[5] that is part of man's psychic structure, not the experiences or ideas themselves. Jung is not a psychological Lamarck. Specific images and formulations are, in effect, symbols for those recurring general ideas. One might say that Jung's concept of the archetype is roughly analogous to the concept of Platonic Ideas. But the Platonic Idea is a model of supreme perfection, which is transcendent and appears on earth only in the form of a representation or copy. On the other hand, Jung's archetype is bipolar in nature and always has a dark, negative aspect as well as a light, positive one. He does distinguish in a rather Platonic way between the nonperceptible, only potentially present archetype and the perceptible, actualized archetypal image,[6] but his archetype is immanent, as the Platonic Idea is not. Jung notes many specific archetypes: the Wise Old Man, the Great Mother, the child, the mandala, the Hero, and so on. Ultimately, however, all archetypes are related to man's psychological struggle to understand and accept his unconscious.

Jung's term for this struggle is "Individuation," and he sees it as having a definite pattern with stages of development common to all men. It can be quite painful and depressing. Once one recognizes the existence of this irrational side (which may express itself in the fearful and rigid adherence to strict rationality, let it be noted), one can begin to accept the more unconscious parts of one's psychic makeup. Individuation is a complicated process with many variations, but in general one may say that the end result is a widened consciousness that accepts and includes the unconscious—although since the unconscious is inexhaustible in its profusion of contents, one cannot really say that one is "individuated" until, perhaps, one is on one's death bed. Part of that expanded consciousness is an acceptance of the inevitability of death as "the individual [is

[5] *Ibid.*, p. 69.

[6] Mary Ann Mattoon, unpublished lectures for "The Psychology of C. G. Jung," p. 24.

brought] into absolute, binding, and indissoluble communion with the world at large."[7] One accepts the world (and one's self), with all of its mutability and chaos.

Archetypal symbols play an important part in this process of individuation, for they "make the transition from one attitude to another possible, without loss of the unconscious,"[8] as opposites are reconciled and one polarity comes to be seen as the reversed face of the other. The archetypal symbols used by the unconscious to this end are of wholeness and perfection, the conjunction of opposites, which is a "paradox . . . characteristic of all transcendental situations."[9] This is the general function of archetypes. More specifically, their appearance to a person in dreams, visions, or fantasies always represents the parts of his psyche from which his ego has dissociated himself. The very force of the archetype makes a person conscious of this previously unconscious part of his psyche. The multiple forms that the archetypes take may seem bewildering at first, but this protean quality is due to the great variety of forms that individuation may take—and it is with this process that archetypes are always connected. Thus an essential characteristic of archetypal symbols emerges: *they are active agents of the unconscious*, dynamically promoting the balance of the conscious and the unconscious.

This persistent interest in the unconscious and the irrational side of existence seems Romantic, as does the central thrust of Jung's psychology, which is so concerned with the development of the individual Self. More importantly, Jung's conception of the mind and its relation to the external world is quintessentially Romantic. He sees the psyche as a "self-regulating system,"[10] or, to put it another way, as an organism with its own internal laws of growth. The psyche is polar, and the internal efforts to reconcile antinomies also shape all of our perception of the external world. Man projects this inner "psychic drama"[11] outwards, and the whole world becomes ar-

[7] Jung, *Two Essays*, p. 178.
[8] Jung, *Structure*, p. 73.
[9] Jung, *Aion*, p. 70.
[10] Jung, *Structure*, p. 79.
[11] Jung, *Archetypes*, p. 6.

chetypal for him, unified by his perception of it. Jung's point
here is the Romantics' point: this predisposition to create ar-
chetypal symbols from the neutral external world because of
the mind's "recurring modes of apprehension"[12] is an essential
characteristic of the human imagination. Jung writes sweep-
ingly, "myths are first and foremost psychic phenomena that
reveal the nature of the soul";[13] Blake writes, rather more
succinctly, "all deities reside in the human breast."[14] The
methodological assumptions of the two are similar, and
the neo-Romantic psychologist may provide insights into the
Romantic poet in a truly heuristic way.

[12] Jung, *Structure*, p. 137.   [13] Jung, *Archetypes*, p. 6.
[14] *The Marriage of Heaven and Hell*, plate 11.

ONE

Myth and Non-Myth

WILLIAM BLAKE struggled with the question of how chaos can be assimilated into imaginative order in all of his works. With his Lambeth Books and Prophecies of the 1790s, he began to address directly this fundamental issue with which all myth may be said to be concerned. These poems primarily attempt to forge a mythos, while at the same time intentionally showing the possible errors into which the mythmaker may fall. They make possible Blake's later centripetal prophecies, themselves "regenerative" of their readers: *The Four Zoas, Milton*, and *Jerusalem*.

Blake's early conception of chaos seems close to the classical Greek one of the primeval Void from whose undifferentiated elements the cosmos was formed, as well as to the alchemical idea of the *prima materia* that awaits the symbolic transmutation of the dark formless matter into spiritualized gold. This conception underlies Blake's cosmogonic poems: *The Book of Urizen, The Book of Ahania*, and *The Book of Los*. But in both his "minor" and his "major" prophecies he came to see chaos as a mythic principle of existence, to be perceived in the horrors of contemporary social circumstance and in the psyche's unexplained unconscious contents. The historical manifestations were only too plain to him from the very beginning of his poetry; but the broader psychological and cosmic implications gradually became apparent to him as well, and his concern to comprehend them became increasingly urgent.

This human compulsion to domesticate chaos (or "Non-Existence" as Blake frequently termed it) by invoking it, reflecting on it, and making human images of it, has always been an important source of mythmaking. There is ever the danger, however, that this all-too-human urge to create order may lead to entropy, manifested in an overly "systematic" poetry as well as a sealed-off attitude to life. Blake became increasingly aware of the problematic aspects of mythic system. His determined lines from the beginning of *Jerusalem* often have been quoted:

> I must Create a System, or be enslav'd by another Mans
> I will not Reason & Compare: my business is to Create.
>
> (*J* 1.10.20-21)

The resulting creation by Los of Golgonooza, the symbolic city of art in Blake's own myth, proves to be paradoxical. Los is creating this "System" in Ulro, "in the depths of Hell" (*J* 1.12.15), and what is strongly suggested is that Los is only creating another fixed dead "System:"

> In pulsations of time, & extensions of space . . .
> With great labour upon his anvils; & in his ladles the Ore
> He lifted, pouring it into the clay ground prepar'd with art;
> Striving with Systems to deliver Individuals from those
>   Systems.
>
> (*J* 1.11.2-5)

A consideration of what Blake says about the properties of "true" art may clarify the nature of the problem just described. In his "Annotations to the Works of Sir Joshua Reynolds," he calls "Non-Existence" the "General" and "Indeterminate," for he was preoccupied in his art, as in his poetry, with absolute clarity of vision. This concern is particularly evident in his belief in the superiority of the "firm and bounding outline" over "tints," "points and dots," and obscuring "lights and shadows": in the firm precision and lucidity of the line rather than the indefiniteness of these other artistic qualities. Even his choice of copper engraving as his metier is significant, since its basic characteristic is strength of line.

When we consider what he has written about the superiority of linear art, we see that he attaches spiritual value to this artistic quality of vision. Thus in *The Ghost of Abel* (1788) he writes,

> . . . Nature has no Outline:
> but Imagination has . . .
> Nature has no Supernatural & dissolves: Imagination is
> Eternity.
>
> (*GA* 1)

In "Annotations to the Works of Sir Joshua Reynolds" (1798) he exclaims, "The Man who asserts that there is no Such Thing as Softness in Art & that everything in Art is Definite & Determinate has not been told this by Practise but by Inspiration & Vision because Vision is Determinate & Perfect." And again, "Singular & Particular Detail is the Foundation of the Sublime . . . Minuteness is [the] whole Beauty [of forms] . . . What is General Nature is there Such a Thing what is General Knowledge is there such a Thing All Knowledge is Particular."[1]

In his comments in *A Descriptive Catalog* (1809), we can see that for Blake the artistic proscription has blended with his most fundamental concerns. He writes: "The great and golden rule of art, as well as of life, is this: That the more distinct, sharp, and wirey the bounding line, the more perfect the work of art; and the less keen and sharp, the greater is the evidence of weak imitation, plagiarism, and bungling. . . . How do we distinguish one face or countenance from another, but by the bounding line and its infinite inflexions and movements? . . . What is it that distinguishes honesty from knavery, but the hard and wirey line of rectitude and certainty in the actions and intentions? Leave out this line and you leave out life itself; *all is chaos again*, and the line of the almighty must be drawn out upon it before man or beast can exist [italics added]."[2]

Yet how much all of this reminds one of that famous drawing by Blake, "The Ancient of Days," in which the main fig-

---

[1] *P & P*, p. 635. [2] *Ibid.*, p. 540.

ure, who is busily outlining the world with his compasses, is—Urizen.

It is psychologically appropriate that those qualities in himself that Blake most disliked would be precisely those projected outward onto the figure of Urizen, and indeed he shows an ambivalent loathing-fascination toward this character. As Jean H. Hagstrum remarks, Blake spends a lot of time in his poetry describing Ulro.[3] Seemingly the archvillain of the myth, Urizen causes man's fall from the company of the "Eternals" in *The Book of Urizen*, and serves as representative of Satan in *America: A Prophecy* and *Europe: A Prophecy*. Yet his history dominates the cosmogonic poems, inextricably interwoven with that of Los, the great creative hero who is the "Eternal Prophet." As will be shown, the story of Urizen parallels that of Los at important points—or is it the other way around?—and the two figures prove to be *complementary* in the Lambeth Books (*The Book of Urizen*, *The Book of Ahania*, and *The Book of Los*). These poems show the beginning of Blake's complex ability to understand the Urizen within himself. As he wrote in *The Four Zoas*:

Startled was Los he found his Enemy Urizen now
In his hands. he wondered that he felt love & not hate
His whole soul loved him

(FZ 7.90.64-66)

Blake seems to have "drawn out . . . the line of the almighty" upon "chaos" to his satisfaction in his art, with the same linear quality remaining characteristic right up until his last "Ugolino with his Sons and Grandsons in Prison," which he completed weeks before his death. But his Lambeth poetry shows an increasingly restless dissatisfaction with the myth that he was trying to construct. The Prophecies show only too plainly Blake's real necessity for myth—the *citizen's* real necessity for myth at that time. The contemporary social horrors, which were to be purged by the American and French

[3] Jean H. Hagstrum, "Babylon Revisited, or the Story of Luvah and Vala," in *Blake's Sublime Allegory*, edited by Curran and Wittreich, p. 400.

Revolutions—at first hoped to be millennial beginnings of
The End—were only deepened as those revolutions provoked
England to declare war on France in 1793. Everything in the
Lambeth Prophecies suggests the belief that there must be fur-
ther pages in God's Book that will show all of this disorder
expunged by some divine scheme.

Yet even when this is said, it must be added that Blake
himself seems to have been aware of the hovering danger of
oversystemization. For the Lambeth Books consciously show
the paradox central to Blake's situation. There is at once the
satiric self-awareness in them of the basic problem of the sys-
tematic thinker, and also the determined reassociation through
myth of that which seems most dissociated in actual experi-
ence. Either may lead to rigidity: in the first case, to a tired
and ironic resignation to the impossibilities of the work con-
fronting the mythmaker; in the second, to a petrifying of the
imagination as the myth becomes fixed. It was truly a gigantic
task that Blake had set for himself but there were quite real
psychological imperatives goading him on, for without perse-
vering he would have fallen either into imaginative death or
experiential dissociation.

If one considers the three Lambeth Books together, one may
see an evolving solution to this paradox. The advance of the
mythmaker (both Blake and Los-Urizen) is painfully won and
precariously kept in them, but it is quite real nonetheless. The
course of events in the later *Book of Los* clearly parallels those
that overtake Urizen in the first three chapters of the earlier
Book of Urizen, but one may measure how far Los has come by
what he is able to make. Urizen's first "dark revolving . . .
silent activity" (*BU* 1.3.18) resulted in his doomed formation
of the "Book of eternal brass"; Los's concluding creation from
his anvils in *The Book of Los* is the sun, the "immense Orb of
fire," which is able to stand "self-balanc'd" (*BL* IV.5.45).
Neither does Los show Urizen's early primitive abhorrence of
"the petrific abominable chaos" in *The Book of Los*, but instead
the promising attitude of *curiosity*.

The Book of Urizen has long been recognized as an "intellec-

tual satire, directed at accounts of cosmic and human genesis
in the Bible, Plato, and Milton."[4] The satire is also directed at
Blake the mythmaker himself. The poem shows a great deal
more than this, of course, and its political and philosophical
place within Blake's thinking has been amply dealt with
elsewhere. But it is surely not an unconscious coincidence that
in the first half of this poem (chapters one through five)
Blake shows all of the various attempts to create system in the
face of chaos, and then devotes the second half (chapters six
through nine) to his *own* systematic account of the begin-
nings of "fallen" time, which cycle toward the historical
present. As he recognizes quite well, such "enormous labours"
must be undergone and Los must "rouz[e] his fires" when man
is "affrighted at the formless unmeasurable death"
(*BU* III.7.8-9). Blake himself plunges on bravely to continue
his mythic account of the Titanic struggle between Urizen and
Fuzon in *The Book of Ahania* after the latter has left Egypt, and
then continues it from Los's point of view in *The Book of Los*.
But the limits of this reaction are shown by its results in *The
Book of Urizen*: Urizen's "Book of eternal brass," Los's creation
of man's material body, the Eternals' curtains and pillars and
woof "round the Void," which is "called . . . Science"
(*BU* V.19.5-9).

The "abominable void," "the soul-shuddring vacuum"
(*BU* I.3.4-5) with which Urizen contends in the beginning of
The Book of Urizen is very like the "Abyss," the "Voidness" of
"non-Entity" faced by all the Zoas and Emanations in the
opening Nights of *The Four Zoas* (which seems to have been
begun around the same time that *The Book of Urizen* was writ-
ten). Blake explores the inward psychological correspondence
to this "Void" in the closing Nights of *The Four Zoas*, and
there is a strong suggestion in *The Book of Urizen* also that this
"vacuum" has its beginnings in the human psyche. In some
curious way, Urizen is its *cause*, since it is he who perceives it
as something to be overcome:

[4] *P & P*, p. 819.

. . . what Demon
Hath form'd this abominable void
. . . Some said
"It is Urizen"

(BU 1.3.3-6)

But it is not a possibility that is developed as fully as in *The Four Zoas*, and in all three of these Lambeth Books the void seems more like an outside condition with which to struggle. The alchemical idea of the *prima materia* which awaits the scientist's transmuting touch is alluded to in *The Book of Urizen*. The "abominable void" is dark, cold, and described by Urizen as "Natures wide womb" (*BU* II.4.16)—all common alchemical designations of it. It is also very like the Greek "Chaos," in which the elements of the universe whirl about dizzyingly, as yet unorganized:

. . . [Urizen] strove . . .
In unseen conflictions with shapes . . .
Of beast, bird, serpent & element
Combustion, blast, vapour and cloud.

(BU 1.3.13-17)

In these two traditions, however, the void is *necessary* to existence, since it contains the elements from which the cosmos (or the philosopher's stone) is to be made. Urizen here sees it as something with which to "str[i]ve in battles dire" (*BU* 1.3.13), and goes on as long as he can with his desperate, churning effort to create order as a defense against the "vacuum." The "Eternals" themselves "avoid The petrific abominable chaos" (*BU* 1.3.25-26). Later, as mentioned, they will build the tent "called Science" against the void. Always in this poem the characters attempt to transcend chaos, or to change it into something different from what it is, and that, as Blake sees quite well, is their essential error. The real God behind the scene (so to speak) rather considers chaos to be a characteristic of "Eternity" in which

> The will of the Immortal expanded
> Or contracted his all flexible senses.
> Death was not, but eternal life sprung.
>
> (*BU* II.3.2-4)

This will prove to be the same vision of the "Regenerated" Albion at the end of Night Nine in *The Four Zoas* who is able to see the height and depth of the universe:

> The Expanding Eyes of Man behold the depths of
> wondrous worlds
> One Earth one sea beneath nor Erring Globes
> wander but Stars.
>
> (*FZ* 9.138.25-26)

But that is a long time away.

Urizen's way of creating order is obviously wrong (he is "unprolific! Self-closd, all-repelling"—*BU* I.3.2-3), and his self-justification in chapter two really a revelation of how obtuse and "un-regenerated" he is at this point. Yet at the same time, his account of his cosmogonic struggle could be Blake's own as mythmaker. Urizen seeks "for a joy without pain, For a solid without fluctuation" (*BU* II.4.10-11). Blake himself celebrates over and over in his poems the glories of an apocalypse that will consume this present anguish and leave only the "desires of ancient times" (*A* 15.25) as "the Grave shrieks with delight, & shakes Her hollow womb" (*SL* 7.35-36); or else he reworks the genealogy of his pantheon, the narrative of his myth, and the cycles of history which have led to the present. The result of all of Urizen's battles with the "void immense" is Urizen's "Book of eternal brass"—and how reminiscent that is of Blake's own engraved books. Of course, Urizen's "Book" with its impossible "Laws of peace, of love, of unity" and its "one King, one God, one Law" (*BU* II.4.34-40) is a warped parody of the Word that really *should* inform the "void." But his impulse still is Blake's own as he writes *The Book of Urizen* in the first place.

The immediate result of Urizen's efforts is the provocation

> The dead heard the voice of the child
> And began to awake from sleep
> All things. heard the voice of the child
> And began to awake to life.
>
> (*BU* VII.20.26-29)

And thus begins the further fall of man that Los had tried to prevent. Fuzon too "groand on the Tree," and in response Ahania is heard, whom Urizen had tried to "hid[e] in darkness in silence" (*BA* 1.2.36):

> The lamenting voice of Ahania . . .
> Her voice was heard . . .
> . . . her tears from clouds
> Eternal fell round the Tree.
>
> (*BA* V.4.45-51)

This final chapter, in which Ahania laments for her lost Urizen, is the emotional core of the Book, and we can begin to comprehend the profound extent to which that erring systematizer is one aspect of the "Eternal Prophet." Ahania makes Urizen an unexpectedly sympathetic character, crying "Ah Urizen! Love! Flower of morning!" (*BA* V.4.52-53) with a real poignancy that only makes him seem "self-destroying" and bound in "chains of darkness" (*BA* V.5.42-43). Granted, this is one central thrust of *The Book of Urizen*: the past nobility of Urizen, which contrasts so grotesquely with his present condition that narrows and narrows. But the effect of Ahania's chant is to draw us into the situation as satire cannot, and her view of him is evidently a dimension to Urizen that Blake saw even as he considered him to be "the Demon" and the "dark power" of Chapter One in *The Book of Urizen*.

Urizen himself has cast out Ahania in chapter one of her Book, and "she fell down . . . wandring in chaos" (*BA* 1.2.38-39). Her reaction to this "chaos" is new in the Lambeth Books, for although she "weep[s] on the verge of Non-entity" (*BA* V.4.53-54), she does not avoid it or try to change it but rather enters into it:

of what he has tried so hard to "close": the "petrific abominable chaos" now seen more clearly as possessing "enormous forms of energy":

> Rage, fury, intense indignation
> In cataracts of fire blood & gall
> In whirlwinds of sulphurous smoke.
>
> (*BU* III.4.45-47)

Urizen in turn runs to seek shelter from the "roaring fires," the "whirlwinds & cataracts of blood" (*BU* III.5.12-13) and frames around himself "a roof . . . like a womb; Where thousands of rivers in veins Of blood pour down the mountains" (*BU* III.5.28-30). He almost seems here to create the first rudiments of the human body, presaging Los's actions.

The two mythic characters act similarly, although Los's "System" will prove somewhat more successful than Urizen's: at least the material body that Los forms does not provoke the destructive rage of the "Eternals," as did Urizen's "Book of eternal brass." Los sets about to create form, just as Urizen did, anguished since his fellow mythmaker "Urizen [is] rent from his side" (*BU* III.6.4) and a "fathomless void" opens beneath his feet. Urizen "fought with the fire" as he struggled in "a void immense, wild dark & deep," writing his laws of consistency "in books formd of metals"; Los too rouses "his fires, affrighted At the formless unmeasurable death" (*BU* III.7.8-9), and binds "every change With rivets of iron & brass" (*BU* IV.8.10-11). Los also is nearly enveloped in the "enormous forms of energy" as "the surging sulphureous Perturbed Immortal mad raging In whirlwinds & pitch & nitre" surges "round the furious limbs of Los" (*BU* IV.8.3-6). The similarity to Blake's own physical labors of engraving the plates of his poetry is quite pronounced here, as:

> The Eternal Prophet heavd the dark bellows,
> And turn'd restless the tongs; and the hammer
> Incessant beat . . .

[Los] heated his furnaces & pour'd
Iron sodor and sodor of brass.

(*BU* IV.10.15-30)

And so Urizen's previous misguided efforts are gathered into the parallel as well.

Man's physical body, which binds "the eternal mind" and "inclos[es] . . . his fountain of thought" is the result, and Blake's extended description of that body subtly makes Los's creation Blake's *own*. The effect of chapter four is rather like a hall of mirrors, with the significance of the action extending forward endlessly: Urizen tries to create "a wide world of solid obstruction" and only causes the "Eternals [to] spurn back his religion"; his failure causes Los to "form nets & gins" and "b[i]nd every change" to the limited form of the physical body; and Blake renders this creation of the body in such a decidedly original way (with his characteristic bite of salt) that once read, it changes the reader's perception of his physical self (and his potentialities) inalterably. The struggle to create myth takes place at all levels, including that of the reader's own imagination.

Blake does not mean to suggest that the "void" is in itself fearsome and destructive, but only that it seems so to those who would change it. As Urizen goes about his brooding war with "the petrific abominable chaos" in the beginning of the Book, Blake describes existence from the other "regenerated" viewpoint:

Earth was not: nor globes of attraction . . .
Death was not, but eternal life sprung.

(*BU* II.3.36-39)

And later in chapter five, after Los has created Urizen's body and stops in horror to view the result, Blake makes it clear that the "enormous forms of energy" *could* be embraced if one had the "all flexible senses" of "the Immortal":

All the myriads of Eternity:
All the wisdom & joy of life:

Roll like a sea around [the newly embodied Urizen]
Except what his little orbs
Of sight by degrees unfold.

(*BU* V.13.28-32)

Then follow Blake's own "secrets of wisdom The secrets of dark contemplation" (*BU* II.4.25-26) as, now caught in the cycles of time and continually pushed forward to the present, Los spawns Enitharmon, then Orc . . . and the genealogy unrolls that is repeated again and again in Blake's later poems.

This history is continued into *The Book of Ahania*, where Urizen experiences the same sexual jealousy toward his son that Los will show when he binds down Orc with the "Chain of Jealousy." Very probably, Orc would have returned the hostility with the same castrating aim of Fuzon. (Fuzon "threw The howling Globe . . . it tore through That beaten mass: keeping its direction The cold loins of Urizen dividing"—*BA* I.2.17-29.) But in *The Book of Urizen*, Orc is still only a "Man child." "Howling, [Orc] with fierce flames Issu'd from Enitharmon" (*BU* VI.19.45-46); Fuzon also appears with "flames" and "sparkles," "roaring with fury" against "this abstract non-Entity" who also happens to be his father. Fuzon disappears from sight forever after chapter four, whereas Orc goes on being born again and again, but here Fuzon further emphasizes the subterranean similarity between Urizen and Los. Los's iron-linked "Chain of Jealousy" bound down Orc after Los watched him grow "fed with the milk of Enitharmon"; Urizen's Disk which "endur'd the cold hammer" as it was "forg'd in mills" is doubled back upon him by Fuzon, who by directing it to "the cold loins of Urizen" reveals that the same sexual fear is working in Urizen that was in Los. Urizen seems like Los to dominate, hurling the rock that "enter[s Fuzon's] bosom" and then nailing him down on the Tree of Mystery just as Los "chain'd [Orc's] young limbs to the rock" (*BU* VII.20.23).

Yet the triumph is only apparent for both fathers. As Orc howls on his rock,

> I lie on the verge of the deep . . .
> I see thy black forests and floods . . .
> Weeping I walk over rocks
> Over dens & thro' valleys of death.
> (*BA* v.4.56-61)

Nor does she deny the reality of what she sees or desperately try to create order, but instead she sings her lament for Urizen as she remembers him. Fear, rage, despair, and jealousy are all that have been known previously. There has been the "Pity" that caused Enitharmon to appear and that parody of sexual consummation, "Man begetting his likeness, On his own divided image" (*BU* VI.19.15-16). Parenthood has only seemed an Oedipal tangle.

But for Ahania, satisfied sexuality causes all existence to take on the luminous "lineaments of gratified desire" (as it will again for the Daughter of Urthona in *America: A Prophecy*). Like the procreating Earth Mother who incidentally creates the world, Ahania

> . . . awake[s] my king in the morn!
> To embrace Ahanias joy
> On the bredth of his open bosom:
> From my soft cloud of dew to fall
> In showers of life on his harvests.
> (*BA* v.5.10-14)

Their resulting children are joyously received and extend her love outward (unlike Orc, the fetal "Worm" who "with dolorous hissings & poisons Round Enitharmons loins fold[ed]"— *BU* VI.19.26-28):

> Swell'd with ripeness & fat with fatness
> Bursting on winds my odors,
> My ripe figs and rich pomegranates
> In infant joy at thy feet
> O Urizen, sported and sang.
> (*BA* v.5.24-28)

Urizen himself, now the husbandman that he will be again in
the apocalyptic Night Nine of *The Four Zoas*, has a unified per-
ception of existence at last as he stands

> . . . with [his] lap full of seed
> With [his] hand full of generous fire
> . . . On the human soul to cast
> The seed of eternal science.

$$(BA \text{ v.} 5.29\text{-}34)$$

Ahania's lament is a vision of the potential regeneration of
human feeling, and she expresses the first authentic notes of
longing, compassion, joy, and love in Blake's cosmogony. It
will be recalled that, according to Hesiod, it was Eros that
harmonized the original Chaos.

And indeed one begins to see a new and richer reaction to
the "void" in *The Book of Los*. This Book seems to take place
sometime after the close of *The Book of Urizen*, for "Eno aged
Mother" is longingly remembering the "Times remote" when
Covet, Envy, Wrath, and Wantonness were dominant—cer-
tainly a fine description of life in "Egypt" before Fuzon called
together the children of Urizen to leave that "pendulous
earth." As one would expect at this point in history, Los is
bound and "compell'd to watch Urizens shadow." Like the
"Eternals" in chapter two of *The Book of Urizen*, who respond
to Urizen's constricting "Laws" with "Rage, fury, intense in-
dignation In cataracts of fire blood & gall," Los "rag'd with
curses & sparkles of fury." There was "no light from the fires"
then and there is none from the fires in *The Book of Los*, either
(*BU* III.4.45-46 and 5.17; and *BL* 1.3.32-49). Los seeks to
burst apart the "vast rock of eternity" in which he is trapped.
It is a prison very like the one known by Urizen earlier. In
chapter two of *The Book of Urizen*, Urizen boasts of having
managed to make "a wide world of solid obstruction"; later, in
chapter three, he flees to hide in "a black globe" when the fiery
cataracts of rage from the "Eternals" seem about to overtake
him. Los himself is caught in "a Solid without fluctuation . . .
Black as marble of Egypt" (*BL* 1.4.4-6). This both refers

backward to the "thirty cities" at the end of *The Book of Urizen*, which are so calcified that Fuzon can only deal with them by leaving them; and also to the actual historical obsidian statues of the Egyptian state, which were theriomorphic, thus (in Blake's eyes) blaspheming against the true divinity of man . . . another effect of Urizen's "Net of Religion."

But where Urizen remained passive to conserve his identity ("Urizen is a clod of clay . . . Cold, featureless, flesh or clay"—*BU* III.6.10 and 7.5), Los bursts free—the "Prophetic Wrath" always managing to avoid entropy at the last. As one would expect, the alternative to that obsidian "Solid" is the "horrible vacuum Beneath him & on all sides round" (*BL* II.4.25-26). Los spirals "in the horrid vacuity bottomless" (*BL* II.4.36), the worst fears of both Urizen and Los thus realized. But a new possibility occurs to Los: why not explore this waste? Blake echoes Milton here, of course, whose Satan explores the deeps in *Paradise Lost*; and this whole scene presages Urizen's later fall in *The Four Zoas* and his resolution to explore the dens of Urthona. Still, this determination to understand the deeps is new for Blake:[5]

> . . . wrath subsided
> And contemplative thoughts first arose
> Then aloft his head rear'd in the Abyss
> And his downward-borne fall chang'd oblique.
>
> (*BL* II.4.39-42)

Rather than "falling" with "incessant whirls," Los now bears "sidelong on the purple air, wafting The weak breeze" (*BL* II.4.47-48) and "with ease search[es] the dire vacuity" (*BL* II.4.53), surely not an unpleasant experience. Urizen simply "strove in battles dire In unseen conflictions with shapes . . . Of beast, bird, fish, serpent & element" (*BU* I.3.13-16); Los

---

[5] To be sure, Blake had enjoyed his sojourn in other deeps in *The Marriage of Heaven and Hell*. But he made his voyage in the present times, and not (like Los) at the very beginning of things. Nor was that "Hell" quite the same as the *materia prima*, "Natures wide womb" (*BU* II.4.17).

performs the infinitely more complex mental act of "incessant
. . . organizing,"

> . . . till the Vacuum
> Became element, pliant to rise,
> Or to fall, or to swim, or to fly:
> With ease searching the dire vacuity.
>
> (BL II.4.50-53)

Los is humanizing the void.

Los created man's body in *The Book of Urizen* just after Uri-
zen, who could not free himself from his "dark globe," seemed
to lie in a "formless unmeasurable death." Here in *The Book of
Los*, too, Blake passes directly from his account of Los's travels
through "the dire vacuity" to Los's creation of the lungs. Here
as there too, there is the quirky dimension of Blakean irony in
the description of these inflatable, deflatable organs that are
"driv'n by waves & englob'd on the tide" (*BL* III.4.58). But
still there is a difference between the passages from each poem,
for the emphasis in the latter is not so much on Los's enclosing
and binding of man's hitherto expansive nature. The lungs
rather are described in terms of the vacuity, almost a further
element of it to be "searched" by Los:

> The Lungs heave incessant, dull and heavy
> For as yet were all other parts formless . . .
> Dim & glutinous as the white Polypus . . .
> . . . the Lungs heave on the wave
> Weary overweigh'd, sinking beneath
> In a stifling black fluid [Los] woke.
>
> (BL III.54-62)

This has the curious effect of making the "vacuity" itself
almost an extension of man, rather than a feared Other with
which to struggle. Los himself sinks; then, into his lungs,
"drew in The spawn of the waters," rising "on the floods"
and with his prophetic "wrath" at last able to separate the ele-
ments of chaos as Urizen was never able to do in the beginning
of *The Book of Urizen*. Los "seperat[es] the heavy and thin," and

at last "Light first beg[i]n[s]" and Los can forge his Sun. Harold Bloom says that Los "creates our fallen world, with its dead sun,"[6] a rather grudging acknowledgment of the myth-maker's accomplishment here. That "dead sun" is made from "those infinite fires" that "glow'd furious in the expanse," and Los views it with the self-satisfaction of an artist who finally likes what he sees:

> Los beat on the Anvil; till glorious
> An immense Orb of fire he fram'd
> Oft he quench'd it beneath in the Deeps
> Then survey'd the all-bright mass . . .
> . . . the Sun
> Stood self-balanc'd. And Los smild with joy.
>
> (*BL* IV.5.33-45)

An emotion he has not shown before!

And yet the poem ends with Blake's irony doubling back upon all of the mythmaking efforts so far: Urizen's, Los's, his own, ultimately. We are left at the end with Urizen, who has now unalterably been given human form ("His Brain in a rock, & his Heart in a fleshy slough"—*BL* IV.5.52-53), finding this created sun yet another torturing restriction as he "lay In fierce torments on his glowing bed." Finally, the "Orb of fire" is only another "Form [that] was completed, a Human Illusion In darkness and deep clouds involvd" (*BL* IV.5.56-57).

The Song of Los apparently continues the history of the Lam-beth Books, since in the Song's beginning "Urizen g[a]ve his Laws to the Nations By the hands of the children of Los" (*SL* 3.8-9). David Erdman has suggested that the two parts of this Song, "Africa" and "Asia," "are built to enclose [*America: A Prophecy* and *Europe: A Prophecy*], the first part to precede and the second to follow them."[7] "Africa" is "pedestrian," as Harold Bloom rightfully remarks.[8] It succinctly recounts his-

---

[6] *P & P*, p. 822.

[7] Erdman, "The Symmetries of *The Song of Los*," *Studies in Romanticism*, 16: 2 (Spring 1977), 179.

[8] *P & P*, p. 818.

tory from the time that Fuzon and the children of Urizen left "Egypt" at the end of *The Book of Urizen* up to the present brink of worldwide revolution. The final line of "Africa" is the same as the opening line of *America: A Prophecy* (excluding the "Preludium"),[9] and so we are invited to read on into that prophecy.

America: A Prophecy and *Europe: A Prophecy* are intensely topical poems, crammed with political allusions to an extent that makes it worthwhile to consider Blake's artistic purposes in using such materials. It has been conclusively proved by Mark Schorer and David Erdman that Blake was deeply involved in radical millennial societies during the 1780s and 1790s. And it is true that these poems might have been written by one of the many millennarians of his own time (assuming some poetic genius in the writer, naturally), since Blake's belief that contemporary history was cycling ever nearer to the eschatological finale was shared by many people then. Certainly one cannot ignore the fact that there is a growing political disillusion in these poems, as Jacobin hopes were dashed and Britain's conservatism prevailed. But still they are more than political poems alone.

One may say that the typical strategy of millennarians has always been to change the perceptions of their readers so that those readers too would stand in the "Last Days" as part of the "remnant of God." But still Blake is attempting in these Lambeth Prophecies to do something beyond all this, something that may be seen as well in his use of contemporary history in his later prophecies, particularly in his conception of Albion, who is both "the Universal Man" and the body politic of England. Of all the Lambeth Prophecies, *America: A Prophecy* succeeds in this attempt the best. Here Blake manages to balance the mythic ordering principle and the outer confusing events that must be ordered by it. The poem shows us the very way in which random historical circumstance is given order, rather than only the finished product of the myth. Blake works to

[9] See Erdman, "The Symmetries of *The Song of Los*," for a fuller discussion of the possible significance of that similarity.

draw the reader into the experience similarly. He uses immediately accessible materials to do so: the public Judeo-Christian millennial myth, the political present, and the universal experience of released sexuality. Ultimately, Blake is trying here to affect the reader's perception exactly as Orc affects that of the Daughter of Urthona in the poem's "Preludium." All of those materials of Orc's vision (which is Blake's own, of course) make it more than the vision of a character in a private pantheon. (For are the actions in *The Book of Urizen* comprehensible if we don't already understand the symbolic significance of the characters and the attitudes that Blake is satirizing?)

The "Preludium" of *America: A Prophecy* is a microcosm of the following "Prophecy," a presentation in terms of Blake's own myth of the change in perception that he intends to produce in the reader. In the beginning, it has overtones of another public mythology—the Norse—as the "shadowy Daughter of Urthona," who is "crowned with a helmet" and armed with a quiver of arrows, brings food to the chained Orc in "iron baskets." Sexuality is the dominant metaphor here and in the rest of the poem, as the Daughter experiences a revolutionary expansion of imagination through an aroused desire. Orc uses as his source of divine energy just those libidinous drives so long repressed by the enemies: that "pale religious letchery" and those "Priests of the Raven." Sexual perception is imaginative perception in *America: A Prophecy*, changing the object to subject and humanizing the whole world so that it attains the "lineaments of gratified desire."

The sexuality in the "Preludium" is incestuous, for Orc and the Daughter of Urthona are brother and sister, since Orc's father, Los, is the generated image on earth of Urthona. The theme of incest, which was common to Romantic literature, is a particularly appropriate one for Blake to use at this point, since incest (especially between brother and sister) archetypally signifies the union of opposites in a religious sense, and is traditionally a prerogative of royalty and divinity. There are myths in which divine incest is said to have produced the universe, and what Blake is describing here is the "coming of the new Heaven and the new Earth" (*Rev.* 21:1) that millennarians always proclaimed.

Their copulation is almost ritual in its anonymity: Orc "siez'd the panting struggling womb" and "*it* [not she] joy'd." Orc "howl[s] his joy" as he gives his vision of "an eagle screaming in the sky, sometimes a lion . . . sometimes a whale . . . anon a serpent" (*A* 1.13-15). The Daughter translates his vision into her own coital experience:

> On my American plains I feel the struggling afflictions
> Endur'd by roots that writhe their arms into the nether
>   deep:
> I see a serpent in Canada, who courts me to his love;
> In Mexico an Eagle, and a Lion in Peru;
> I see a Whale in the South-sea, drinking my soul away . . .
>
> (*A* 2.10-14)

Orc's creatures are phallic and political at the same time, referring simultaneously to the act of copulation and to slave revolts in America, abortive historical rebellions, and the "South Sea" scandal of British commerce. This radicalization of vision in the Daughter is due to her orgasmic "limb rending pains," "eternal death" (surely the Elizabethan pun here), and "torment."

The "Prophecy" itself is pungently immediate from its very beginning. We must recall the setting in which it would have been read, for to a great many Englishmen (and Americans) the current events seemed almost hysterically confusing. We are plunged directly into the maelstrom as "Washington, Franklin, Paine & Warren, Gates, Hancock & Green" summon up the present experience of those caught in the British workshops and the British ships of commerce and war, whose "faces [are] pale and yellow," whose "hands [are] workbruis'd," whose "feet [are] bleeding on the sultry sands," and who know the "furrows of the whip" (*A* 3.9-11). These Americans confront "the Guardian Prince of Albion," the contemporary George the Third.

This actual experience shared by the readers of the poem becomes the ground for the myth as Orc appears on plate 3 in answer to Washington's rebellious voice. Orc's ascent over the Atlantic is distinctly sexual, and he thus seems a figure from common psychological experience. The vision of Ezekiel at Chebar is Blake's source, but the source is transformed. In Ezekiel's vision, a man appears ("the likeness of the glory of the Lord") in the midst of the "living creatures" who seem to be "a wheel in the middle of a wheel": this man is "amber, as the appearance of fire round about it, from the appearance of his loins even upward, and from the appearance of his loins even downward . . . and it had brightness round about" (*Ezek.* 1:27). This sounds much like Orc, who

> Red rose . . . from the Atlantic in vast wheels of blood
> . . . a Wonder o'er the Atlantic sea;
> Intense! naked! A Human fire fierce glowing, as the wedge
> Of iron heated in the furnace; his terrible limbs were fire.
>
> (*A* 4.6-9)

In Ezekiel's vision the fire that appears about the man obscures his loins; in Blake's vision, the fire *is* Orc and Blake stresses his nakedness. There is also the phallic implication in the rising Orc's being compared to "the wedge of iron heated in the furnace."

Plate 6 is a traditional apocalyptic prediction, with images that could be taken from the most ancient accounts: "the morning comes . . . the grave is burst . . . the bones of death . . . reviving shake . . . breathing! awakening! . . . the Sun has left his blackness, & has found a fresher morning." This terminology is continued in plate 7, as the tyrannical "Albions Angel" calls Orc the "Antichrist," for this ironic reversal of the truth is typical behavior of the true Antichrist during the "Last Days." Orc's answer to this "Angel" is like the vision that he declared to the Daughter of Urthona, combining at once the reference to the private myth ("the fiery joy [returns] that Urizen perverted to ten commands"), the public apocalyptic myth ("to make the desarts blossom, & the deeps shrink to their fountains . . . Fires inwrap the earthly globe, yet man is not consumd"), and the universal psychological experience ("that pale religious letchery, seeking Virginity, may find it in a harlot . . . The undefil'd tho' ravish'd in her cradle night and morn").

Plates 9 and 10 again draw the reader into the actual political circumstances, more insistently seen in terms of Blake's myth as the "thirteen Angels" of the American colonies begin their rebellion and Enitharmon's "Harlot womb . . . heaves in enormous circles" to give birth to this latest manifestation of Orc according to Blake's cycles of history. The "thirteen Angels" plot their rebellion in "the Colonies" on plate 10; and then on plate 11 there is again the fiery immersion in all of the terrible political circumstances of British commercialism, imperialism, and utilitarianism. As the historical confusion and the mythic structure interweave in the remainder of the poem, there is no longer any separation between them as each is interpreted in terms of the other.

Like "A Song of Liberty," *America: A Prophecy* concludes with the falling of empires as the Revolution spreads from America to Europe and the "Last Days" come. The Americans are "naked & flaming," and presumably about to enjoy

> . . . the females naked and glowing with the lusts of
>   youth . . .
> [Who] feel the nerves of youth renew, and desires of
>   ancient times,
> Over their pale limbs as a vine when the tender grape
>   appears.

(A 15.22-26)

Man finally possesses Orc's sexual and revolutionary vision:

> . . . the five gates were consum'd, & their bolts and
>   hinges melted
> And the fierce flames burnt round the heavens,
>   & round the abodes of men

(A 16.22-23)

America: A Prophecy was written before England's counter-revolutionary war against France in 1793, when it appeared that perhaps the American Revolution would spread to Britain, and so was the "Signal of the Morning which was told us in the Beginning" (*J* 4.93.26). By the time that Blake was writing *Europe: A Prophecy* in 1792-1794, it had become a distinct possibility that the forces of reaction in England were stronger than the forces of revolution, and that Albion himself was going to war to suppress Orc's ascension in France. Both with picture and text, plate after plate of this latter poem show the contemporary horrors that call for the cleansing fire. The conflagration of "the fierce fires" that burnt off all sensuous and political restraints in the concluding plate of *America: A Prophecy* has become "the strife of blood" at the end of *Europe: A Prophecy*; further, it is inevitable and necessary, leading as it will to the "Last Days" of the millennium. This apocalypse itself has gained dark undertones that answer to the increasingly menacing political situation, which is the immediate setting for the prophecy. These "Last Days" may leave "the five gates . . . consum'd"; they will also be bloody and violent. In France's Reign of Terror innocents were in fact drawn in the tumbrils as well as aristocrats, as Blake knew.

In *Answer to Job*, Jung provides a penetrating psychological analysis of millennarians coming to terms with chthonic visions from the unconscious;[10] and *Europe: A Prophecy* as a whole resembles those apocalyptic visions of the unconscious mind that Jung analyzes. Jung wrote of the visions of vengeance and destruction that the devoutly Christian John of Patmos spent so much time describing, "as a totality, the self is by definition always a *complexio oppositorum*, and the more consciousness insists on its own luminous nature and lays claim to moral authority, the more the self will appear as something dark and menacing."[11] Certainly there is an abundance of imaginative energy connected with all of those dark visions (in John and in other writers as well). The terrors of the "Last Days," the Last Judgment, and the coming of the wrathful Son of God all clearly have their roots in very real emotions and psychological

---

[10] Jung, "Answer to Job," in *Psychology and Religion: West and East*, 2nd edition.

[11] *Ibid.*, p. 443.

states. Of course, the dragon is finally bound at the end, and
the demon finally consumed by fire. For such writers it would
seem that the possibility of such an imminent apocalypse ex-
plained all that had seemed alien in their own personal experi-
ences. Writing of the apocalypse reunified themselves as well
as the world.

Sexuality as a dominant metaphor may seem to be absent
from *Europe: A Prophecy*, for Orc's sexual-apocalyptic fires have
disappeared, and so have his "glowing," "naked & flaming"
sympathizers. Actually this metaphor also pervades *Europe: A
Prophecy*, but in a different form. Sexuality in *America: A
Prophecy* was largely a metaphor for revolutionary triumph, and
the sexually aroused female was essentially a passive object of
male delight. The Daughter of Urthona in its "Preludium"
was a virgin who stood "dumb" and "silent" until Orc seized
her, and her sexuality was submissive as she received the phal-
lic thrusts:

> On my American plains I feel the struggling afflictions
> Endur'd by roots that writhe their arms into the nether
>   deep . . .
> . . . thy fire & my frost
> Mingle in howling pains, in furrows by thy lightnings
>   rent.
>
> (A 2.10-16)

The "naked & glowing females" at the end of that poem expe-
rienced only the preliminary stage of sexual arousal, only a be-
ginning engorgement "over their pale limbs as a vine when the
tender grape appears."

By contrast, the female sexuality in *Europe: A Prophecy* is
frenzied and aggressive. The "shadowy female's" description of
birth in the "Preludium" seems to corroborate the opinion of
some psychologists that giving birth is similar to orgasm. In
her own mother Enitharmon's song later in the poem, the sex-
ual female is tyrannic:

> Now comes the night of Enitharmons joy! . . .
> That Woman, lovely Woman! may have dominion . . .

. . . & from her childhood shall the little female
Spread nets in every secret path.

                                        (E 6.1-9)

The story of the "shadowy female" is continued from its be-
ginning in *America: A Prophecy*. In that poem, she had en-
visioned the necessity for revolutionary liberation; but in
Europe: A Prophecy, she sees the realization of that liberation
with its attendant horrors. Further, whereas in the "Prelu-
dium" of *America: A Prophecy* she was initiated into sexuality,
in the "Preludium" of *Europe: A Prophecy* she is in the resulting
throes of childbirth. This image may derive from chapter 12 of
Revelation, but the "shadowy female" is more than an image
that Blake borrowed from the Bible. Medusa-like, she appears
with "her snaky hair brandishing in the winds of Enitharmon."
Medusa has strong associations with the unconscious. To
Freudians, she symbolizes a threatening vagina crowned with
pubic hairs. Jungians prefer to see her less specifically as sym-
bolizing the treacherous, ambiguous unconscious that can only
be dealt with when viewed by the mirror of rational conscious-
ness.

At any rate, the "female's" speech is savage as she tells of her
revolutionary sons that she constantly brings forth as "howling
terrors, all devouring fiery kings," bound to eat up the Euro-
pean monarchs who are in their way. "Mother Enitharmon,"
the "Queen of Heaven" who probably here represents the re-
pressive and proscriptive British AntiJacobin forces, may try
to "stamp with solid form this vig'rous progeny of fires . . .
stamp[ing] them with a signet" (2.8-10); but this only pro-
vokes the "shadowy female" to display her true chthonic na-
ture more openly. In the line "I wrap my turban of thick
clouds around my lab'ring head" (E 1.12), there is a hint that
she is connected with those capped Jacobin women who sat
watching the guillotine during the Reign of Terror. And do
the following lines suggest the mother of Pentheus who, mad-
dened by Dionysus, tore Pentheus limb from limb as she wan-
dered with the other bacchantes over Thracian mountains? We
know that Blake read Greek drama.

> Devouring & devoured roaming on dark and desolate
>   mountains
> In forests of eternal death, shrieking in hollow trees.
>
> (2.5-7)

The force that she lets loose has an energy that seems uncontainable. She cries:

> And who shall bind the infinite with an eternal band?
> To compass it with swaddling bands? And who shall
>   cherish it
> With milk and honey?
>
> (2.13-15)

One might think that Blake would feel that the political climate which was trying to stifle the revolution was equally inchoate: we know from his other works its terrible daily effects on "Albion's" citizens. Significantly, however, Blake chooses for the rest of the poem to give form to that political present by recasting it in terms of the cycles of history which have led up to those times. He devotes a large proportion of *Europe: A Prophecy* to his mythic explanation of the sources of present-day corruptions, something he did not do at all in *America: A Prophecy.* Thus misery is given point. It is the familiar story of the history that has always before been recounted in the face of "the soul-shuddring vacuum" or "the dire vacuity": Enitharmon falls asleep to dream an eighteen-hundred year "Dream" of the centuries from Christ to the present; she awakes to call her children; and as her son Orc arises, the world revolution is reaching all the thrones of Europe.

Significantly, Blake's description of Enitharmon and her children (all of whom, save Orc, are associated with the enemy to be repelled) compares them to objects that are shifting and many-hued, and thus lacking clear form. So Enitharmon's house is prismatic "crystal," Manathu-Vorcyon has "flames of soft delusion," Leutha is winged like the "many colord bow" with her daughters "many changing revolv[ing] like sweet perfumes," and Antamon is "prince of the pearly dew." All of this anticipates Blake's later aesthetic statements on the superiority of the "firm and bounding outline."

With the final plate we are back in the chthonic world of the "shadowy female" of the "Preludium." The first eight lines are full of allusions to the French Revolution: "red [Jacobin] France," "the furious terrors," the tumbril-like "golden chariots raging, with red wheels dropping with blood"—lines that could as well be from the viewpoint of the victim as of the rising Orc. These golden chariots might be those that Orc has used in *America: A Prophecy* when he rose over the Atlantic "in vast wheels of blood," but the wheels here *drip* with blood. Are the wheels red because they reflect the apocalyptic fires, or are they red because they have run over men? Is there a difference? "The Tigers couch upon the prey & suck the ruddy tide"—and is that anonymous "prey" monarch or unfortunate citizen? The relish with which those animals finish up even the blood suggests that the question of righteousness makes no difference to them either. Los lifts his head "in snaky thunders clad," now assuming the appearance of the "shadowy female" as well as her ferocity. There obviously should be an Armageddon in the very near future.

The historical-geographical sequence leads from *America: A Prophecy* and *Europe: A Prophecy* to *The Song of Los*. "Asia" of this last poem recapitulates the situation: the horrors of the political climate are to be seen everywhere, and only the traditional millennium can change things. Bloom notes that "throughout 'Asia' one can feel Blake's poetic relief, as he ceases to catalogue disaster, and turns instead to admonition and prophecy";[12] and certainly that is an accurate reaction to this last half of *The Song of Los* and (if we accept Erdman's plausible suggestion) this concluding Lambeth Prophecy. But there is a "poetic relief" as well in the passionate denunciation of those disasters, which recalls the painful cry of Ahania as she stumbled "alone over rocks, mountains . . . Where bones from the birth are buried Before they see the light" (*BA* v.5.39-47). It

[12] *P & P*, p. 819.

is a "relief," because the hidden pattern to this historical dis-
order has been revealed finally, as it was not to Ahania. All of
the horrors of plate 6 in "Asia" now turn out to be merely the
prelude to what is coming at the end of plate 7—a rendering of
the apocalypse in all of the old images: the dusty bones that
rise to join together, the clay that again becomes flesh, the
grave that gives birth, the sudden revitalization of the land-
scape. Carrying out his own earlier sexual motif from *America:
A Prophecy*, Blake makes that yonic grave turn from an aged
woman ("the Grave shrieks with delight," which sounds like
the cackling of an old hag) to one in her experienced prime of
life ("her bosom swells with wild desire") to one who is in her
early child-bearing years ("milk & blood & glandous wine In
rivers rush & shout & dance"). But still, the traditional images
suggest the essentially traditional myth underlying this
flourishing conclusion to the immediate circumstances.

The Lambeth Books worked out the central paradox of the
mythmaker, with Blake "striving with Systems to deliver"
himself "from those Systems." The Lambeth Prophecies show
us where the problem really lay for Blake: in the *nature* of the
millennium as he conceived of it then. All through his matur-
ity, he wrote and rewrote his vision of what the apocalypse will
be like, that mythic event which perhaps more than any other
shows an imaginative control of existence as divine order rises
to conquer chaos in all forms: the oppressive rulers of empires,
the wicked of this world, the fallen angels who inhabit this
world, and ultimately Satan himself. Writing of the apoc-
alypse over a period of years, Blake takes us closer and closer to
the center of the event. In his Prophecies of the 1790s, he
never takes us beyond the bloody violent "Last Days" that are
the prelude, although we can guess that it will prove the kind
of millennium usually portrayed: the prelapsarian era will be
restored with God's order once again informing all of the uni-
verse. Night Nine of *The Four Zoas* goes further, through the
"Last Days" into the dawning of the "regenerated" perception

of Albion when (as the final line of the entire poem tells us) "sweet science reigns." It remains for the last three plates of *Jerusalem* to enter into that actual "reign," giving us "the Visions of God in Eternity" (*J* 4.96.43), which turn out to be very different from what they would have been if Blake had proceeded beyond the conclusions of *America: A Prophecy*, *Europe: A Prophecy*, and *The Song of Los*. For those Prophecies were quite within the Judeo-Christian millennial tradition, however fast and loose with it Blake played. So an understanding is necessary of that tradition within which Blake was working, even if what he was really doing was working free of it.

The eschatological event itself has been consistently apprehended since at least the second century B.C. The creator of apocalyptic visions has always believed that he stood in the "Last Days," days which in their very horror, injustice, and violence show that this world cannot be redeemed as it is but needs a complete reversal if God's will is to be manifested. The imagery and symbolism of these visions is stylized. Almost always there is a great combat between the Divine Creator with his angels and the Antichrist with his demons, a judgment of the unrighteous after Christ's victory at Armageddon, and unremitting torments visited upon the wicked, the tyrannical, and the unjust, all described with relish by the millennarian (who usually came from the downtrodden religious minorities). This Antichrist was usually portrayed as a great sea monster, a dragon, or a snake, and the events of the "Last Days" frequently seemed surrealistic.

Mircea Eliade has shown how fixed is this view of history, which sees all mankind progressing from one point in time (God's creation of this world) to the final point in time (God's transformation of this world and His imposition of another perfect and righteous world order).[13] According to Judeo-Christian apocalypticism, "the End of the world will occur only once, just as the cosmogony occurred only once . . . . Time is no longer . . . circular . . . it has become a linear and

[13] Eliade, *The Myth of the Eternal Return*.

irreversible Time."[14] Chaos in all of its present historical man-
ifestations is something to be transcended at the end and
purged out of existence as God's reign finally prevails.

In the Prophecies following those written at Lambeth, one
can see Blake's dawning realization of the limitations of this
mythic viewpoint, and his growing conviction that chaos may
be a polarity of the cosmos after all. For certainly the non-
myth—non-Being, sheer confusion—haunts his Lambeth in-
terpretation of contemporary history like a photographic nega-
tive. In these millennial Prophecies, the intrinsic limitations
of the Judeo-Christian *schema* become increasingly obvious. If
Blake is to convince us that history is about to be ended, he
must show us all the present historical manifestations of the
non-myth that will be canceled: monarchical tyranny, the
"stony law" of religion (*A* 8.5) that is prevalent, the utilitar-
ians and Malthusians who set the policies of the State (*A*
11.8-15), the proliferating censorship laws (*E* 12.5-8), the
growing paranoia of uncontrollable power (*E* 12.26-31), and
Newtonian materialism (*E* 13.4-8). One cannot help recall-
ing that historically the millennial hope was strongest when
events seemed most hopeless and confusing to the Jewish or
Christian writer. What does one do with all of these materials
outside the myth if they are not ushering in the "Day of the
Messiah" but rather are simply present conditions under which
one has to live?

The Marriage of Heaven and Hell was written slightly before
these Prophecies, but it too shows Blake's conflicting ap-
prehensions of the millennium. The conclusion of what is ap-
parently the poem proper suggests the possibility that the
apocalypse may be something other than a last cataclysmic
event as "the Angel . . . stretched out his arms embracing the
flames of fire & . . . was consumed and arose as Elijah," with
the Angel and Devil "often read[ing] the Bible together in its
infernal or diabolical sense" (*MHH* 24) in an apparently con-
stant mental apocalypse. This anticipates Blake's comment in
A Vision of the Last Judgment that "whenever any Individual Re-

<hr>

[14] Eliade, *Myth and Reality*, pp. 64-65.

jects Error & Embraces Truth a Last Judgment passes upon that Individual."[15]

But then in the immediately following "A Song of Liberty," Blake seems to return to the old idea of the "Last Days" that are about to usher in the millennium. Here again he lists all of the awful contemporary phenomena: the "dungeon" of France, the papal empires of "old Rome," the commerce of London, the slavery endured by the black African, the monarchical tyrannies of Europe, the religious "stony laws" of the Mosaic "ten commands." The Song begins at the precise moment when it is revealed that these are but variations on one mythic truth: the world is controlled by agents of the Antichrist and can be cleansed only by the violence of the "Last Days."

Significantly, these agents are shown here as passive and fearful, lacking the fiery vitality of Orc and his forces who finally vanquish them. (Later, in *The Four Zoas*, the Antichrist will not appear so feeble.) The monarchies face Orc and the "hoary element roaring fled away . . . falling, rushing . . . buried in the ruins"; and the contemporary manifestations of the Antichrist in the Chorus are "the Priests of the Raven of dawn" who simply "with hoarse note curse the sons of joy," his brethren who "lay the bound," and the "pale religious letchery [who] call that virginity, that wishes but acts not." These adversaries of Satan have none of the horrible power of evil that the adversaries of God had in the usual apocalyptic accounts, and that made the final triumph over them so significant of the ultimate power of God's order over chaos. But if Blake felt that outer disorder was otherwise overwhelming, it becomes understandable that he would portray the forces of evil as being so passive. If he had a private sense of engulfing historic circumstance, he would have had to make the powers of Orc that invincible and dynamic.

It was near the end of this Lambeth period that Blake's poetry took a dramatic new turn, as nearly all his critics have noticed. For the first time, Blake gathered together the elements of his myth that had previously been scattered through his works into one massive poem, beginning as *Vala* around 1795 and ending as *The Four Zoas* around 1808. He had been struggling toward this formulation for at least the past decade. Startling in mythic conception and splendid in poetic power as many of the Lambeth poems are, one senses a discontent in them as Blake starts but never quite finishes his projects. But he kept at *The Four Zoas* for at least ten years before he finally left it, still in manuscript form. In this poem, Blake first articulates his full myth of man's fall from a "perfect unity" with "the immortal One" into a complete psychological dissociation, and then his "Regeneration by the Resurrection from the dead" (*FZ* 1.4.5). This "Regeneration" is now placed considerably in the future, and Blake is more concerned with the interactions among members of his own pantheon than with the European monarchs and counsellors of his 1790s Prophecies. With *The Four Zoas* he began writing his "major" prophecies, which were all impressively longer than anything he had done before: where *America: A Prophecy* and *Europe: A Prophecy* are 18 plates long, *The Four Zoas* is 139 pages long, *Milton* is 50 plates long, and *Jerusalem* is 100 plates long. His metrics changes, too, as he adopts the long line of seven feet. Clearly, Blake's major prophecies are unlike anything he has written before.

There are several critical interpretations of this change in Blake's poetry. There are those who hold that his poetry reflected the radicalism of his time, and that as England grew more conservative Blake began hiding his true revolutionary tendencies by using the private symbolism of his myth to conceal his real opinions about contemporary events. Erdman is perhaps the most prominent and influential of these critics.[16] For during the very early 1790s, it became clear to most that the apocalypse was not going to begin in Europe (as many believed was literally happening). Hope turned to despair, and popular millennarianism ended with English AntiJacobinism and the onset of the Napoleonic wars. England became increasingly reactionary as the war dragged on, even Napoleonic, and

---

[16] Erdman, *Blake: Prophet against Empire*.

Romantic poets generally lost faith in the millennium as a political event.

Others think that when Blake saw that an actual political millennium was not coming, he retreated to the solace of the purely mental apocalypses of *The Four Zoas*, *Milton*, and *Jerusalem*. Blake becomes for these critics one of the first modern poets who must create what Earl R. Wasserman calls a mythic "syntax" because there is no satisfactory public one. As Wasserman says, "In Blake's day man could have a System—a new language with its symbols and special syntax—only by forging it for himself."[17]

Finally, some think with G. E. Bentley that Blake underwent a conversion to an intensely religious Christianity, a religious process given considerable impetus by historical circumstances. Bentley, the editor of the facsimile text of the manuscript of *The Four Zoas*, draws this conclusion as he notes that the religious allusions in *The Four Zoas* appear to be late additions.[18]

I would suggest another interpretation: that the change was due to reasons that were more internalized than the above critics would imply. It will be my argument that Blake's conception of the relationship between myth and non-myth, order and chaos, changed in his poetry, if not in his art. When he was writing *America: A Prophecy*, it seemed that social disorder was about to be consumed in the greater movement toward universal harmony that had begun. He still had the embers of this hope alive when he wrote *Europe: A Prophecy* and *The Song of Los*, although one can tell from the growing chthonic quality of that anticipated apocalypse that he knew it was not going to happen soon. And as this became clearer to him from outward events, he found it imperative to understand the very nature of chaos if he were to know how to deal with its presence in "Albion." *The Four Zoas* proceeds beyond the Lambeth

---

[17] Wasserman, *The Subtler Language*, p. 12.

[18] Bentley, *Vala or The Four Zoas*, p. 165. But see David Erdman, "The Binding (et cetera) of *Vala*," *The Library*, 19 (1964), for criticism of Bentley's conclusions on this point.

Prophecies to inquire into the psychological sources both of man's sense of disorder and his impulse to order it, Blake going more deeply into the mythopoeic process than ever before in his poetry. There he begins to move towards a dynamic myth that manages to incorporate the formless non-myth. To put it another way, *consciousness begins to incorporate the unconscious.* Myth and non-myth will merge in *Jerusalem*, but (incredibly) Blake will be able to preserve the polarity of chaos as part of his myth.

My general approach to Blake's poetry is Jungian, which may seem unorthodox to some students of English literature, but not, I think, to Blakeans. Blake himself was eclectic, since he thought that all areas of human endeavor show the effects of the human imagination. As mythmaker, he was encyclopedic, drawing upon Western philosophic and religious traditions, as well as upon his contemporary history and science. Jung's own psychology was rooted not only in clinical experience but in a scholarly background similar to Blake's, including as it did ancient mythology, alchemy, Gnosticism, and neo-Platonism. Why may not a critic follow Blake's very approach to knowledge, using discoveries from fields of human experience such as depth psychology, comparative mythologies, and anthropology? Modern discoveries in these disciplines were unknown to Blake, yet they have as the object of their study man's perception and imagination, just as Blake's poetry does.

If Blake did not have at hand the abstract principles of modern depth psychology, certainly his knowledge of human psychology is in harmony with many of the later findings of Freud and Jung. The subject of all Blake's poetry was "the Universal Man['s] . . . fall into Division & his Resurrection to Unity" (*FZ* 1.3.6—4.4); what changed was his conception of how that "Resurrection to Unity" was to be achieved. This essentially is also the history of modern depth psychology, as well.

Blake's constantly reiterated assumption was that poetry arises out of the dynamic process of the imaginative life, and that the reader may share in that life by "Enter[ing] into these Images . . . on the Fiery Chariot of his Contemplative

Thought," as he wrote in *A Vision of the Last Judgment*.[19] Jungian psychology can help the literary critic to understand *how* literature is an ongoing imaginative experience since, according to Jung, archetypal symbols are dynamic, affecting and altering the psychological contexts in which they occur. In reaching his conclusions, Jung produced materials about archetypal symbolism that can prove of real value for the literary critic who wishes to understand how such symbolism acts in literature. Indeed, in my course of "mak[ing] a Friend & Companion of . . . these Images of wonder"[20] in *The Four Zoas*, I hope to reach some conclusions that might lead me toward the formulation of a critical theory based on Jungian psychology.

The Four Zoas is certainly not the same as the Lambeth poetry that precedes it, but that is because a different mythos informs it. Traditional millennarianism is basically dualistic. Its dualism is not the metaphysical dualism of spirit and matter, but the belief in two opposing cosmic powers—God and Satan—and two ages—the present irretrievably evil age under Satan, who now oppresses the righteous, and the future perfect age, when God will rule and the righteous will be blessed forever. This dualism underlies the Lambeth Prophecies, whether Blake was conscious of it or not, and that was the root of his problem.

For if one considers his work as a whole, it is difficult to think of a less dualistic writer than Blake. The eschatological culminations of his major prophecies give us the *coexistence* of these powers:

The Expanding Eyes of Man behold the depths of wondrous
    worlds
One Earth one sea beneath nor Erring Globes wander but
    Stars
Of fire rise up nightly from the Ocean & one Sun
                      (*FZ* 9.138.25-27)

---

[19] *P & P*, p. 550.   [20] *Ibid.*

. . . terrific Lions & Tygers sport & play
All Animals upon the Earth, are prepard in all their
    strength
To go forth to the Great Harvest & Vintage of the Nations
                              (M II.42.38—43.I)

All Human Forms identified even Tree Metal Earth &
    Stone. all
Human Forms identified, living, going forth & returning
    wearied
Into the Planetary lives of Years Months Days & Hours
    reposing
And then Awaking into [Jesus'] Bosom in the Life of
    Immortality.

                              (J4.99.1-4)

This later view sees all existence informed by the constant
interplay of polarities, rather than leading towards the final
triumph of the one polar principle of Goodness, or Order.
Alan Watts defines this interplay as well as anyone: "Polarity
. . . is something much more than simply duality or opposi-
tion. For to say that opposites are *polar* is to say much more
than that they are far apart: it is to say that they are related and
joined—that they are the terms, ends, or extremities of a
single whole. Polar opposites are therefore *inseparable* oppo-
sites."[21] This was not a mythic viewpoint that suddenly sur-
faced in *The Four Zoas*, for Blake had expressed it vigorously in
The Marriage of Heaven and Hell with his doctrine of "Con-
traries." But still the body of that poem is followed by "A
Song of Liberty," *America: A Prophecy*, *Europe: A Prophecy*, and
The Song of Los. Blake began to explore that mythic possibility
again in his major epics (all of which seem to have been begun
about the same time), impelled both by the outward circum-
stances already mentioned and by inward ones to be discussed.

It might seem that this concept of "Contraries" had ap-
peared earlier in Blake's works, most notably in *The Songs of*

---

[21] Watts, *The Two Hands of God: Myths of Polarity*, p. 49.

Innocence and Experience, which purport to "shew . . . the Two Contrary States of the Human Soul." Thel, too, in her Book is invited to move from her initial State of Innocence to its contrary State of Experience in "the land unknown" which may lead eventually to a higher "redeemed" State; and when Oothoon (unlike Thel) follows this invitation in *Visions of the Daughters of Albion*, she eventually does become spiritually liberated. Yet the word "Contrary" is not being used in the same sense in those poems that it is in *The Marriage of Heaven and Hell*, for these "Contrary States" are not really related as are the polarities.[22] Blake observes in this latter poem that "the Prolific would cease to be Prolific unless the Devourer as a sea recieved the excess of his delights" (plate 16). But there is nothing beneficial at all about the State of Experience (except perhaps that it arouses one's "Prophetic Wrath"), as there is about the "Devourer." Experience only deadens everything. Nor is it dependent upon the State of Innocence, as the "Devourer" is upon the "Prolific" (and *vice versa*). Innocence is simply blighted by Experience and becomes something different from what it was originally, unlike the Contrary of the "Prolific."

Much has been written about Blake's dialectic of Contraries in *The Marriage of Heaven and Hell*.[23] Early in the poem, Blake holds that "without Contraries is no progression. Attraction and Repulsion, Reason and Energy, Love and Hate, are necessary to Human existence. From these contraries spring what the religious call Good & Evil. Good is the passive that obeys Reason[.] Evil is the active springing from Energy. Good is Heaven. Evil is Hell" (plate 3). It becomes clear in the course

[22] *The Tyger* is a glaring exception to my generalization, as complete a symbol of this balance of polarities as one can imagine. There, indeed, the Creator made the Lamb and equally made the Tyger—both at the same time and in the same place. The surrounding Songs are still sung from the incomplete State of Experience so that the poem itself stands "in the forests of the night," about to catch the reader by the throat.

[23] Martin K. Nurmi's analysis of what Blake meant by Contraries in *The Marriage of Heaven and Hell* remains the most comprehensive. Nurmi, *Blake's "The Marriage of Heaven and Hell": A Critical Study*.

of the poem that Blake is writing about something more than a mere dialectic of opposites, for these Contraries are, as Watts says, *"inseparable* opposites." Blake writes somewhat later in the poem, "The roaring of lions, the howling of wolves, the raging of the stormy sea, and the destructive sword. are portions of eternity too great for the eye of man" (plate 8). These are *permanent* elements of "eternity" which ideally are to be comprehended by man imaginatively and not transcended by him. (For they may be "too great for the eye of man," but when has Blake ever said that man is to be limited by what he can see?)

It becomes apparent still later in *The Marriage of Heaven and Hell* that this "dialectic" is really *enantiodromia*, the state in which everything turns inevitably into its opposite. Thus neither polarity can be cast out ultimately, and there is the intimate (if usually unspeakable) relationship between the two of which Watts writes. "Thus one portion of being, is the Prolific. the other, the Devouring . . . Some will say, Is not God alone the Prolific? I answer, God only Acts & Is, in existing beings or Men" (plate 16). So God Himself must be balancing these polarities, for if the "Devourer" is necessary for the existence of the "Prolific," then it is necessary for God as well. This seems as far from the usual millennial conception of God as one can get: that bone-crunching "roaring of lions [and] howling of wolves" and that "destructive sword" are part of the very order of things, and not just a temporary Armageddon.

It is necessary here to distinguish between the sword that is part of political conquest, and the sword that has more cosmic associations of purification, sacrifice—and liberation. I am *not* saying that Blake thinks military warfare and British imperialism to be "portions of eternity," or that acceptance of the polarity of chaos entails acceptance of the social horrors he sees around him in "Albion." Quite the opposite. But those circumstances can only be eliminated by fully comprehending their source. "The destructive sword" in *The Marriage of Heaven and Hell* is one of a series of elements suggesting wrath, strength, the freeing of energy.

This mythic viewpoint reaches maturity in *The Four Zoas*. He never engraved an authoritative edition of this first major prophecy, and it has been rather neglected critically. Yet it is too important to leave alone, for in it Blake breaks free from that paradox which faced him in the Lambeth Books and Prophecies. The shift in his mythic outlook I think to be due not so much to external accidents of history as to the psychological experience of the mythmaker who finds his system tightening into entropy. It is the very experience of Orc, who takes on the magnificently jeweled but constricting coils of a serpent when he confronts the monolithic and "un-regenerated" Urizen in Night Eight of *The Four Zoas*.

TWO

The Balance of Archetypes
in *The Four Zoas*

IT might seem at first that the political aspects of "regeneration" are not as germane to *The Four Zoas* as they are to Blake's earlier poetry. The millennium is seen as an imminent historical possibility in the Lambeth Prophecies, and more as a psychological event in *The Four Zoas*. Here, Blake gives us "the torments of Love & Jealousy in the Death and Judgement of Albion the Ancient Man" as that "Man's" psychological faculties try to work together to achieve the final "Resurrection from the dead" (1.4.5). But Blake's very designation of this Adam Kadmon, this Everyman, this archetype of the Self, as "Albion" tells us that Blake wants to remind us that the poem concerns his homeland, at the very least. *The Four Zoas* marks Albion's first appearance as a major character, and he figures prominently in the drama of *Jerusalem* as well. So it is quite clear that Blake's insistent desire to include the social dimension of existence in his myth has its roots in something more profound than the typical wish of any writer to base his art in experience.

This is, of course, apparent in Blake's earlier poetry as well. The conviction prevailing there is that somehow mythic order *must* be created because of the nature of immediate historic events. Other people *must* be made to see things as Blake does (if necessary, as Orc made the Daughter of Urthona share his vision in *America: A Prophecy*) in order to clear the circumstantial life of that error which threatens to destroy all goodness and all humanity. But in that earlier poetry there are so many conflicting elements interwoven with Blake's use of radical politics: the subsuming of the historical into the very private go. The possibility of psychosis as the ego is caught up and consumed is always present. The unconscious is beyond the controls of rational order, and man's first reaction in confronting it is, in fact, panic. "The unconscious no sooner touches us than we *are* it," says Jung.[5]

Jung analyzes the two neurotic reactions to the unconscious: either dissolution of consciousness as the ego identifies with the unconscious, or the attempt to "control" the unconscious by imposing order upon it and strangling its very real existence. The third possible reaction is the one that Jung considers to be psychologically healthy: the *acceptance* of the unconscious by consciousness. Archetypes play active roles in this acceptance, for if they may remind a person of what has been repressed into the unconscious, they may also help to protect him when that unconscious seems overwhelming and psychic disintegration inevitable.

These are exactly the dual functions that archetypes perform in *The Four Zoas*. As has been mentioned, archetypes of the unconscious are prominent in the poem as Blake investigates those repressed chthonic realities at which *Europe: A Prophecy* only hinted. The unconscious comes to be seen as part of a larger totality, and by the conclusion of Night Nine the "portions of eternity too great for the eye of man" are finally part of Blake's vision; the darkness enlightened while retaining its polar quality. Gradually, as the Nights progress, these archetypes of the unconscious come to seem *related* to archetypes of the Self. Typically, these latter archetypes appear in a person's dreams or fantasies to remind him of the possibility of psychic unity even in the face of immediate psychological chaos. And so these archetypes act here.

The descent into the unconscious is the general course of action for all of the Zoas and their Emanations. At first, only the negative aspect of the unconscious is apparent; gradually, its positive side emerges as well. The true "Regeneration" in the

[5] Jung, *Archetypes*, p.22.

mythology which, one might think, would act as a barrier to the ordinary reader's understanding; the consistently self-ironic portrayal of the problems involved in creating any order in the first place; the use of the Judeo-Christian mythological heritage to express the necessity for a revolutionary overturning of tradition.

However, before there can be a reunification of the body politic, there must be a complete understanding of the psychological declivities from which that destroying error proceeds. If, as Blake writes in *The Everlasting Gospel*, "Thou art a Man God is no more Thy own humanity learn to adore" (52-54:75-76), then it is equally true that "Satan is no more," either. This correlation between the psychological and the social "regeneration" to come emerges as a major theme in *Milton*, where Blake turns to examine his own satanic sources, which must also be "adore[d]." The social dimension of *Milton* helps to prevent the poem from simply being a demented picture of megalomania (along with other, more complex ways of prevention to be discussed in the next chapter). The outer events *demand* a culture hero. Blake must become the Bard for others as well as for himself, and there are all the horrors of contemporary life to justify his assumption of Milton's "stance." In *Jerusalem*, one visage of the "Devourer" is but the reversed face of the other: inner and outer chaos both explored in all their "Minute Particulars." Blake only begins to consider this relationship in *The Four Zoas*, where he is more occupied in daring to explore for the first time the full psychological implications of "Voidness" and "the soul-shuddring vacuum." But still, never in any of Blake's poetry is there a retreat inward to some esoteric perfection, but rather the constant expansion outwards to all of "Albion."

We have peripheral evidence about the period when Blake was writing *The Four Zoas, Milton,* and *Jerusalem*. It was apparently a crucial period in his life, although he was never very explicit about why this was so. In 1800, he set out for his ill-fated three years' stay at Felpham. Thus the poems were being written in part while he endured the poetaster Hayley's famed solicitude and "soft dissimulation of friendship" (M 1.8.35); and also during the period immediately following, when he returned to London and discovered that "a Man almost 50 Years of Age, who has not lost any of his life since he was five years old without incessant labour & study,"[1] could not find steady employment as an engraver. And it was also a time of increasing national conservatism as Britain intensified its war with Napoleonic France. Recalling those years afterward, Blake declared of them, "I have indeed fought thro' a Hell of terrors & horrors (which none could know but myself) in a Divided Existence."[2]

One would expect that the poetry of this period would provide some internal suggestions about the nature of this "Divided Existence" and "Hell of terrors & horrors." Significantly, The Four Zoas is concerned with Albion, whose warring "faculties" are personified by the Zoas, themselves separated from their Emanations. The poem thus is a study of the experience of "Divided Existence." Further, the main enemy faced by Albion, Zoas, and Emanations alike is "non-Existence." Blake may call it "the Abyss" or "Voidness," but it is the same quality of existence that draws his attention in each case: the formlessness of chaos, everything that is outside the compass of imaginative order.

In the Lambeth Prophecies, this "non-Existence" tended to assume outward social forms. In America: A Prophecy, it is manifested in war and materialism, and also in forms of superficial order that mask profounder disorder: tyrannical government and legalistic, institutionalized religion. Europe: A Prophecy suggests obliquely that this social chaos may originate in human nature and thus be indestructible. Blake faces this possibility directly in The Four Zoas. In the opening lines of Night Two, Urizen "stood in the Human Brain" looking at the sleeping Albion and "mighty was the draught of Voidness to draw Existence in" (2.24.1). This "Voidness," rather than kings,

___

[1] The Letters of William Blake, edited by Geoffrey Keynes, p. 78.
[2] Ibid., p. 109.

counsellors, or priests, terrifies the Zoas and throughout the poem.

Grasping the essential similarity between the ma of Blake's "Voidness" and Jung's archetypes of the sharpens the outlines of the psychological process in The Four Zoas: consciousness is trying to comp unconscious without being overwhelmed by it. conception of the poem amply bears out a psych terpretation of it. The main characters themselves logical "faculties" of the sleeping Albion, and all tions take place during his nine-night dream. Enitharmon near the beginning:

. . . in the Brain of Man we live, & in his circl
. . . this bright world of all our joy is in.the Hur
(1.

Few Jungian critics have considered the poem, ceptions of June Singer and W. P. Witcutt.[3] Bot poetry to speculate about the psychology of the the poetry, about whom we know, in fact, very critics who have discussed Blake's attitude towar scious as revealed in his poetry generally write i vein; they see Blake calling out in his earlier p freeing of libidinous energy and a celebration of s ure and the "fires of Orc." Orc thus becomes representative of the id,[4] and Blake's "hell" in T Heaven and Hell is a symbolic portrayal of the un

The unconscious in Jungian psychology is not to be understood or so easily assimilated, howev as it does the collective as well as the personal un Jung, the unconscious can never be fully compreh sciousness, "heaven" never completely married t would such a total marriage be desirable. The Janus-faced, and while it can be a source of creat can also threaten the very existence of the small

___

[3] See Singer, The Unholy Bible; and Witcutt, Blake: A P
[4] Randel Helms, "Orc: The Id in Blake and Tolkien."

poem begins when Los is able to use the energy of the uncon-
scious to build Golgonooza in Night Seven, working with his
newly reconciled Emanation to construct that "city of art" in
the "nether heavens" (7.87.8). But this is possible only after a
long exploration of the nature of this "nether" world by all the
Zoas.

The descent begins soon after the poem opens. In Night
One, Tharmas first "sunk down into the sea a pale white corse"
(1.5.13); Enion follows and gives birth to Los and Enithar-
mon, who "repel . . . her away . . . into Non Entity" (1.9.5-
6); Los and Enitharmon hear the chthonic "Nuptial Song" at
their marriage feast; Enion chants her terrible "Lamentation";
and finally, at the Night's conclusion, Urthona, Urizen, and
Luvah "sudden down fell . . . all together into an unknown
Space Deep horrible without End" (1.22.38-39). The Emana-
tions seem to have the clearest insight into the nature of the
new realm into which they have fallen in this Night, for the
Zoas do not quite comprehend what is happening to them:
they fall but seem numbed. It is the Emanations who wander,
lament, exult, despair.

The Emanations as characters independent of their consorts
have been neglected by critics, although they play an important
psychological role in *The Four Zoas*. The general critical inter-
pretation of them is perhaps best summed up by S. Foster Da-
mon, who says that "the Emanation is the feminine portion, or
'counterpart,' of the fundamentally bisexual male . . . . The
separated Emanation [separated from her Zoa] . . . acquires a
will of her own, which by definition is turned against her con-
sort."[6] Not all view her only negatively, seeing the important
Emanation Jerusalem as well as Vala. Some have gone further
to claim that the Emanations are the animae of their Zoas,
which seems like an inadequate interpretation.[7] (The anima in
Jungian psychology is a personification in a symbol, or in an
actual human being, of those aspects of his unconscious of

---

[6] Damon, *A Blake Dictionary*, pp. 120-21.
[7] Singer, *The Unholy Bible*, p. 212; Witcutt, *Blake: A Psychological Study*,
pp. 43 ff.

which a man is most ignorant, usually his emotional, irrational qualities.) True, the Emanations pertain to the unconscious, but if they were simply animae they would have characters as differentiated as those of their Zoas. They are more than projections of their Zoas, coming to seem like forces rather than mere "feminine portions" of the Zoas. Indeed, if one considers all four Emanations together, one may see that they comprise the archetype of the Feminine, with the bipolar qualities characteristic of the archetype: two representing the positive side (Ahania and Enion), and two the negative (Vala and Enitharmon). They act together for their Zoas precisely as Jung says such an archetype acts upon a man, leading him toward a knowledge of his unconscious that his manly "consciousness" tends to obscure.

Enion is the first Emanation to appear, and (as Ahania will also prove to be) she is associated with a nurturing goddess of childbirth and motherhood. In Enion's case, that goddess seems to be Demeter. Her search for her children Los and Enitharmon in pages 8 and 9, and for Tharmas in the larger context of the whole poem, corresponds to Demeter's search for Persephone. It is not contradictory to point out that Tharmas, whom she loves so yearningly, may also be compared to Poseidon (consort of Demeter), for in Night Four Tharmas disappears into the sea "on his furious chariots of the Deep" (4.52.7). Demeter assumed the disguise of an old woman as she looked for Persephone in her wandering upon the earth, and Enion too has a "blind, age-bent" appearance throughout the poem. As she follows her truant children in Night One, "her hair became like snow on mountains . . . her bright Eyes decayd . . . in pangs of maternal love" (1.8.8—9.3). We do not see her again until the end of this Night, but her great chants later in this Night and in Night Two (1.17.1—18.7 and 2.35.1—36.13) could be those of Demeter wandering upon earth and gaining a knowledge of mortality and mutability (and a corresponding compassion for man) that she never knew as an Olympian.

Of all the Emanations, Enitharmon acts most like her Zoa's

anima. She has the anima's hypnotic fascination for Los. Intimately attuned to his hidden fears, she is both teasing and vindictive as she initiates her Zoa into a knowledge of those desires that have been repressed into the personal unconscious. Her first appearance in Night One predicts the pattern into which she and Los fall during the next six and a half Nights:

> Alternate Love & Hate [in] his breast; hers Scorn & Jealousy
> In embryon passions. they kiss'd not nor embrac'd for
> shame & fear.
>
> (1.9.24-25)

She predicts her future behavior:

> To make us happy let them weary their immortal powers
> While we draw in their sweet delights while we return them
> scorn . . .
>
> (1.10.3-4)

And later, at their nuptial feast in Night One, the newlyweds sit "in discontent & scorn" (1.13.19).

This "golden Feast" (1.18.8) is the occasion for the first declarations of what is to be seen in this process of descent: the horrors of "Non-Existence." It repulses human order much as does the Contrary of the "Devourer" in *The Marriage of Heaven and Hell*. Those "portions of eternity" to be seen in the realm of the "Devourer" are the subject of the epithalamian sung by the "Demons of the Deep," and their "Song" is Blake's first sustained surge of prophetic vision in the poem. Full of allusions to contemporary warfare, commerce, industrialism, and Newtonian physics, it deepens the significance of the poem immeasurably, drawing the reader into the "Deeps," too. It is followed immediately by Enion's chant of essentially the same things, but with the important difference that she is anguished by what she sees.

By page 18 of the first Night, Zoas and Emanations have all "fallen" one by one "in a fierce hungring void" (1.22.41); and as if in answer to this, the Night closes with archetypes of the Self in the form of three distinct mandalas: the Council of

God, the seven eyes of God, and the yonic vision by the Daughters of Beulah on page 20.

The mandala is an "archetype of wholeness"[8] and much of its significance in Jungian psychoanalysis lies in the patient's experience of creating it. "Mandala" is the Sanskrit term for "circle," specifically the circle in religious symbolism that concentrates attention on unity, wholeness, and centeredness.[9] Jung first encountered mandalas in Eastern philosophical texts, and also found them emerging spontaneously in the drawings and dreams of his patients. The effect of both the mandalas of religious symbolism and those of his patients seemed the same: "Their basic motif is . . . a central point within the psyche, to which everything is related, by which everything is arranged, and which is itself a source of energy. . . . This centre is not felt or thought of as the ego . . . but as the *self*. [This] is surrounded by a periphery containing everything that belongs to the self—the paired opposites that make up the total personality."[10]

All mandalas express the idea of order and balance. Many take the shape of rotating spheres; other mandala motifs are gardens, eyes, wheels, cities.[11] The vast majority of individual mandalas have as their center the Anthropos, or Universal Man. They are more than mere artistic motifs, however, and Jung says that mandalas are useless for patients when produced consciously and artificially. When made spontaneously, they can hold a personality together in times of great stress. Generally appearing in dreams or fantasies when a person is experiencing the worst kinds of dissociation, they attempt to unify seemingly irreconcilable elements. This is characteristic even of what Jung calls "disturbed" mandalas—"disturbed" because they reveal attempts to exclude what Jung calls "the dark principle." Such attempted mandalas fail to symbolize the psychic totality of the true mandala that incorporates *all* parts of the Self—the unprincipled and formless unconscious as well as consciousness.

[8] Jung, *Archetypes*, p. 388.   [9] *Ibid.*, pp. 355 ff.
[10] *Ibid.*, p. 357.   [11] *Ibid.*, p. 361.

These mandalas at the conclusion of Night One are all successful in form and function. Here the Council of God, which "behold[s] as One Man" (1.21.3-4), "Elect[s] . . . the Seven Eyes of God . . . the Seven . . . one within the other" (1.19.9-11). This clearly echoes Ezekiel's vision at Chebar of "four living creatures [with] the likeness of a man," joined wing to wing and moving on wheels with "rings full of eyes round about them four" (*Ezek.* 1:5-18). As it happens, Jung writes about this particular vision, commenting that if the symbol of the vision of multiple eyes "appears in monadic form as a single . . . eye, it readily assumes the shape of a mandala and must then be interpreted as the self."[12]

This casts light on the Council of God. Pages 19, 21, and 22 show us that the Council appears after Enion laments the existence of "Eternal Death," summing up the story of the Zoas' fall. The Council "dr[aws] up the Universal tent . . . & closd the Messengers in clouds . . . Till the time of the End" (1.19.7-9), suggesting that the apparent chaos that the Zoas are experiencing is part of a larger pattern of order known to the Council. To give form to this order, the Council sets up the Seven Eyes of God with "the Seventh . . . named Jesus" (1.19.11).

Jesus at the heart of the mandala is significant. From his early to his late poetry, Blake is consistent in his view of Christ as symbolic of the whole man, an *imago dei* that is yet essentially human. Jung thinks that Christ represents human totality, saying that "the spontaneous symbols of the self . . . cannot in practice be distinguished from a God-image."[13]

In *The Four Zoas*, mandalas appear when the "Abyss" or "Non Existence" seems overwhelming to a Zoa or Emanation. The Council of God appeared when "Eternal Death" seemed dominant to all. Page 20 follows the Council's appearance: the attempt by the Daughters of Beulah which, if she were to have intercourse with Los (when he "should enter into Beulah thro her beautiful gates"—1.20.7), would become a fulfilled mandala having at its center the *hieros gamos*, the divine marriage of

[12] Jung, *Structure*, p. 199.   [13] Jung, *Aion*, p. 40.

sexual opposites that Jung considers another archetype of the Self.

Night Two opens with Albion passing the "Sceptre" of authority to Urizen, who first rises "exulting . . . from the [Nuptial] Feast," and then realizes with sickening horror the true nature of the psychological process that is happening as he "st[ands] in the Human Brain" (2.23.12). He sees "the Abyss" around which Enion wanders, and "Mighty was the draught of Voidness to draw Existence in" (2.24.1). Urizen stands with "his feet upon the verge of Non Existence" (2.24.4), and, "his soul shrunk with horror," he builds the Mundane Shell. This revolving sphere is a geometrically shaped enclosure having the form of a mandala:

> . . . twelve halls . . . composd
> The wondrous building & three Central Domes . . .
> Each Dome opend towards four halls & the Three Domes
>   Encompassed
> The Golden Hall of Urizen.

> (2.30.15-21)

It rotates through the "Abyss," with his sons and daughters outlining its circumference as they travel "in silent majesty along their orderd ways In right lined paths outmeasurd by proportions of number weight And measure. mathematic motion" (2.33.22-24). But it is a mere husk of a mandala as the "worlds" within move on paths that are "Trapeziums Rhombs Rhomboids Paralellograms . . . In their amazing hard subdued course in the vast deep" (2.33.34-36). At its center is the antithesis of the Anthropos, a Druidical altar built by "ten thousand Slaves," where Ahania and her sons are practicing human sacrifice. It is like the Mundane Shell on pages 24 and 25, which Urizen builds when he confronts the "Abyss," having at *its* center the tormented "Luvah cast into the Furnaces of affliction & sealed" (2.25.40).

Luvah falls into his own characteristic form of the unconscious, consumed by ceaseless libidinous fires in the furnaces. He will not appear again until Night Nine, and the last sight of him before that finale is in Night Two. Here he is "quite melted with woe" and becomes a "molten metal" which is let out of the furnaces to run "in channels" for the Sons of Urizen to use in building the Mundane Shell—an interesting anticipation of the modern psychoanalytic theory of repression which sees repressed libidinous energies being channeled into socially acceptable molds.

Luvah's portrayal of Vala here as an "Earth-worm" who grows from a "scaled Serpent" to a "Dragon winged bright & poisonous" (2.26.5—2.27.20) is our first direct sight of her. The serpent in Blake frequently appears as the uroboros. Although Blake's drawing of Vala here does not picture her as that snake with its tail in its mouth, she seems distinctly serpentine, and was apparently conceived by Blake as the alchemical *materia prima* of Nature that was traditionally emblemized as a poisonous dragon.[14] It should be stressed that another alchemical emblem of the *materia prima* was the uroboros.

Jung and his prominent follower Erich Neumann have materials on the uroboros that cast significant light upon Vala. In *Psychology and Alchemy*, Jung compares transmutation to individuation, the "philosopher's stone" that the alchemist strove to discover being in reality his own fully individuated Self. The undifferentiated *materia prima* from which this "stone" was transmuted was psychologically the projected unconscious of the alchemist.[15] If to this interpretation of alchemy we add Neumann's analysis of the beginning stages of the ego's development, we may see the role played by Vala. Neumann considers the infantile ego to be caught in the world of the unconscious and dominated by the symbol of the womb-like uroboros in this dawning stage of psychological development.[16] The uroboric Great Mother comes to seem sinister to the ego only when the ego tries to free itself from the power of the unconscious. Rather than being the uterine round which

---

[14] Piloo Nanavutty, *"Materia Prima* in a Page of Blake's *Vala,"* in *William Blake: Essays for S. Foster Damon,* edited by Alvin H. Rosenfeld.

[15] Jung, *Psychology and Alchemy,* 2nd edition.

[16] Neumann, *The Origins and History of Consciousness.*

nourishes and sustains life, the uroboros seems to the struggling ego more similar to the dragon-like Terrible Mother who is impregnated by her lover-son and then castrates or kills him.

Psychologically in the poem, Vala acts the role of the uroboric Great Mother who threateningly holds her son in the grip of the unconscious. Jung would call her a "Devouring Mother." Throughout the poem, Luvah is encompassed in the fiery round of the "Furnaces of affliction & sealed" as the embryo is in the womb, and those furnaces endlessly burn like the sexual fires of the libido. Vala's reaction to his imprisonment is that of the mother whose lover-son has tried to break away:

> Vala incircle[d] round the furnaces where Luvah was clos'd
> In joy she heard his howlings, & forgot he was her Luvah
> With whom she walkd in bliss, in times of innocence &
>   youth.
>
> (2.26.1-3)

As Luvah describes her, Vala has hermaphroditic characteristics, as many "Terrible Mothers" in mythology have.[17] Luvah's memory of her is couched in distinctly phallic terms:

> . . . I calld forth the Earth-worm from the cold & dark
>   obscure
> I nurturd her I fed her with my rains & dews, she grew
> A scaled Serpent . . .
> [Till] she became a Dragon winged bright & poisonous.
>
> (2.27.7-13)

This phallic serpent appears later when Ahania says:

> Vala shall become a Worm in Enitharmons Womb
> Laying her seed upon the fibres soon to issue forth.
>
> (3.38.8-9)

---

[17] So to the infant, both breast and milk seem generative as well as parturient, as the protruding breast is aggressively thrust into the child's receptive mouth and the milk "fertilizes" the child.

Blake draws Vala on page 27 as a dragon with a phallic tail, emphasized vulva, and multiple breasts (this last characteristic also common to mythological portrayals of the Great Mother goddess).

Luvah's rebellion seems as much against her as against Urizen. Luvah's fall after he challenges Urizen is generally seen as a case of the emotions trying to gain control of the intellect, but it also shows the effort of the ego to escape unconsciousness and develop a greater individual consciousness. Luvah's recollection of Vala reveals a struggle for independence from the "Devouring Mother" archetype, what Neumann calls "the phallic stage . . . of ego development"[18] which strives for freedom from the maternal archetype through "male-chthonic phallicism": subordination of her through copulation. Luvah's memory of Vala as he burns is bitter and intensely sexual, and Hagstrum is surely right in recognizing elements of sexual perversion in Luvah's description of her, elements even more obvious in accompanying drawings of Vala in the manuscript.[19] Much has been erased, but enough remains to make it clear that Blake drew her in coital positions more familiar in Babylon than Beulah (as John Grant notes).[20] Luvah cries from his furnaces, "reasoning from the loins" and still dependent on her:

> . . . I suffer affliction
> Because I love. for I was love but hatred awakes in me . . .
> . . . O when will you return Vala the Wanderer.
>
> (2.27.13-20)

As Luvah fades from sight in Night Two, there are again visions of the chaos that seems to be spreading on earth, and Urizen and his Sons continue work on their "Mundane Shell."

[18] Neumann, *The Origins and History of Consciousness*, pp. 306 ff.

[19] Hagstrum, in Curran and Wittreich, eds., *Blake's Sublime Allegory*, pp. 108-10.

[20] John E. Grant, "Visions in *Vala*: A Consideration of Some Pictures in the Manuscript," in Curran and Wittreich, eds., *Blake's Sublime Allegory*.

Enitharmon, the other manifestation of the negative aspect of the archetype of the Feminine, voices her anima-wisdom and further acquaints Los with the darker, sadistic "torments of Love & Jealousy" in 2.34.57-92. Her "Song" of the "birds & beasts" which "seek for [their] mate[s] to prove [their] inmost joy" and "furious & terrible . . . sport & rend the nether deeps" (2.34.71-73) reveals the energy of this savage "portion of eternity." As a character, she passes beyond her rather petty and squabbling previous nature; and she almost gains the bloodthirsty dignity of some chthonic earth goddess:

> The joy of woman is the Death of her most best beloved
> Who dies for Love of her
> In torments of fierce jealousy & pangs of adoration . . .
> Now my left hand I stretch to earth beneath
> And strike the terrible string
> I wake sweet joy in dens of sorrow . . .
>
> (2.34.63-65 and 83-85)

Enion answers Enitharmon as she answered the "Demons of the Deep" at Enitharmon's nuptial feast in Night One, and her chant which closes Night Two is one of the most memorably poignant passages in the poem. Blake himself almost seems to write of his own bitter and lonely experience:

> What is the price of Experience do men buy it for a song
> Or wisdom for a dance in the street? No it is bought with
>   the price
> Of all that a man hath his house his wife his children
> Wisdom is sold in the desolate market where none come to
>   buy.
>
> (2.35.11-14)

Enion's chant awakens Ahania so that "never from that moment could she rest upon her pillow" (2.36.19), and the two thus become connected in sympathy. Her vision is echoed by Ahania in Night Three as Ahania sees "Eternal Death" in "dark futurity," an experience seeming very distant from what Urizen knows upon his "starry throne." As consort of the

Zeus-like Urizen, Ahania is comparable to Hera. Hera was originally a goddess of childbirth and nature, like Demeter; Ahania is also associated with change and the rhythms of nature, and, in her vision in Night Three, with the necessity for acceptance of these aspects of reality. She sees the error of Urizen's coldly intellectual concept of "holiness":

> Then Man ascended . . .
> Above him rose a Shadow from his wearied intellect
> Of living gold, pure, perfect . . .
> A sweet entrancing self delusion, a watry vision of Man . . .
>
> (3.40.1-5)

Like Enion, she is sensitive to the "Death of Man," and all of the roiling human emotions:

> . . . the Human Heart where Paradise & its joys abounded
> In jealous fears in fury & rage . . .
>
> (3.42.11-12)

And, like Enion, Ahania is anguished by this insight into the human misfortune, and knows the importance of accepting its existence. As she warns Urizen, "Listen to her who loves thee lest we also are driven away" (3.42.8). This frightens Urizen, who expels her exactly as the overly conscious, overly "masculine" male rejects in fear any feminine elements in his own being. Later he recalls her in water imagery, the imagery of flux and flow:

> . . . Once [she was] in my breast
> A sluggish current of dim waters. on whose verdant margin
> A cavern shaggd with horrid shades. dark cool & deadly.
>   where
> I laid my head in the hot noon . . .
>
> (3.43.12-15)

Later in Night Six, when he meets his daughters, these women are also associated with rivers, "mistress[es] of these mighty waters." They will not be compelled to obedience any more than Ahania was, and when he casts them out with his curse he falls (as he does in Night Three after casting out Ahania) into a bitter new knowledge of how ineffectual is pure consciousness as he beholds "the ruind spirits once his children" (6.70.6) acting as he decreed.

Urizen's own fall is described more extensively in *The Four Zoas* than that of the other Zoas. In the opening lines of the third Night he is the "King of Light . . . high upon his starry throne," a perfect representation of the rigid ego that will only recognize consciousness. The vision of his Emanation emphasizes the unruly, irrational side of existence ("intoxication from the wine presses of Luvah"—3.39.6). When Urizen casts her out, he exclaims, "Art thou also become like Vala" (3.43.5), which reveals the extent of his own ignorance. Of all the Emanations, the tender Ahania is actually the least like Vala. So it is just that Urizen falls "into the Caverns of the Grave & places of Human Seed," a literal fulfillment of Ahania's vision of the "Death of Man." It is a cold, congealed place reminiscent of Urizen's own icy "petrific" qualities. But even here there are latent regenerative powers. Blake describes the "Caverns" as "places of *Human Seed* . . . a world of Darkness . . . Where the impressions of Despair & *Hope* enroot forever" [italics added] (3.44.3-5).

Tharmas, who has already fallen as a "pale white corse" into the sea, bursts into speech at this point and shows the extent to which he has become part of the primeval ocean. He is the "parent power" who represents the "faculty" of Sensation, and he cries:

> . . . Fury in my limbs. destruction in my bones & marrow
> My skull riven into filaments. my eyes into sea jellies
> Floating upon the tide wander bubbling & bubbling
> Uttering my lamentations & begetting little monsters.
>
>   (3.44.23-26)

An obvious symbol of the unconscious, the sea is an appropriate setting for Tharmas, as it is reminiscent both of the blood coursing through the body and of the amniotic fluid that orig-

inally rocked us all. Tharmas remains a formless figure in the
poem, dwelling in the sea and riding "the dark Abyss"
(4.47.1).

Urizen continues falling in Night Four, losing any vestige
of consciousness as he sleeps "in a stoned stupor in the nether
Abyss . . . freezing to solid all beneath" (4.52.20-23). "Ter-
rified Los beh[o]ld[s] the ruins of Urizen beneath A horrible
Chaos to his eyes" (4.52.11-12), and Los creates a material
body for Urizen yet once again. In *The Book of Urizen*, this mis-
taken act ultimately resulted in the fallen society of the pres-
ent: "Egypt," as Fuzon rightly saw. Here, the reference to the
dissociated present is more oblique, for Los's creation is fol-
lowed by a shift in perspective as:

> The Corse of Albion lay on the Rock the sea of Time &
>   Space
> Beat round the Rock in mighty waves & as a Polypus
> That vegetates beneath the Sea the limbs of Man vegetated
> In monstrous forms of Death a Human polypus of Death.
>   (4.56.13-16)

This passage functions on several levels of meaning, for the
chaos that is made palpable in the figure of Albion is both so-
cial and psychological. The fears of the Zoas and Emanations
within the poem are finally realized, for the horror of this
"Human Polypus" is that it once was "the Universal Man" but
now is without any identity of any kind. One would think that
Albion's "sons and daughters" reading the poem might feel
some similar terror.

Yet, very significantly, this all occurs *within* the framework
of another mandala, for the "Council of God" sees all this hap-
pening and Christ descends to the decaying Albion. There is
more than a hint that within this "corse of death" may lie the
possibility of regeneration, that life may even exist within
death. On the political level, may not a society that once con-
sidered itself "Christian" possess at least the potential for re-
turning to that archaic vision? As usual, Blake said it best:

And did those feet in ancient time.
Walk upon Englands mountains green:
And was the holy Lamb of God,
On Englands pleasant pastures seen!

(*M* 1.1.1-4)

And in the narrative of the poem itself, Albion's limbs "vege-
tated In monstrous forms of Death" like the "polypus that veg-
etates beneath the Sea." This suggests a vast formless organism
to be sure, but one which is *alive* and perhaps even capable (as
it vegetates) of feeding those "little monsters" of the deep that
Tharmas claimed to "beget" as he fell in Night Three.

Equally important is Christ's reaction to this "Human
Polypus of death," for it represents an attitude to chaos that is
new in *The Four Zoas*:

The Saviour mild & gentle bent over the corse of Death
Saying If ye will Believe your Brother shall rise again
And first he found the Limit of Opacity & namd it Satan
In Albions bosom for in every human bosom these limits
    stand
And next he found the Limit of Contraction & namd it
    Adam.

(4.56.17-21)

Jesus does not fear this manifestation of "Non-Entity" as did
the Zoas and Emanations, but rather attempts to incorporate it
into his perception. "Mild and gentle," unafraid of the engulf-
ing influence of the polypus, Jesus states that both "Limits"
coexist in man. If man has the imagination to "believe" in
Christ the archetype of Self, life will "rise again" out of death,
social harmony out of fragmentation, the individual con-
sciousness out of the unconscious.

It is not an attitude that Los is yet able to embrace, al-
though he will be able to at the end of Night Seven. He alone
of all the Zoas has not yet descended into the unconscious, and
at this point the vision of the "Human polypus of Death" only

creates in him a greater terror. Night Four ends with him, maddened, "stamping the Abyss" and as resistant to it as any of the other Zoas were before him.

As he dances in the fallen world at the beginning of Night Five, his great Oedipal rival is born, and his Emanation begins his real initiation into a knowledge of his repressed desires. Orc is born, and Los's jealousy grows as Enitharmon cares for the boy. She seemingly is unaware of what is happening and makes no effort to reassure Los of her affection for him. The imagery in this passage is a curious reversal of the "primal scene" fantasy as the father imagines the son mating with the mother in the night:

> Enitharmon nursd her fiery child in the dark deeps
> Sitting in darkness. over her Los mournd in anguish
>   fierce . . .
> . . . a tightening girdle grew
> Around [Los's] bosom like a bloody cord.
>
> (5.59.25-26; 5.60.10-11)

Enitharmon sees "how with griding pain [Los] went each morning to his labours" (5.60.20-21), but still she shows her clear preference for her "lovd joy" who is Orc.

Los is the generated form on earth of "dark Urthona," who seems identified with the underworld. Los himself is constantly building and forging from the ores of the earth. He first falls into his personal unconscious. After he carries Orc "shuddring & weeping thro the Gloom & down into the deeps" (5.59.24), Los repents and wanders deeper through "the Gloom of Entuthon Benithon" (5.62.15) pitying Orc with "Despair & Terror & Woe & Rage" (5.63.4) and falling deeper and deeper into the earth. The "Chain of Jealousy" connects Los and Orc from this point on, and Orc's experience becomes Los's own. Los's descent thus goes down to those Caves of Orc "where love shall shew its root in deepest Hell" (5.65.12), into the substratum that is the collective unconscious.

Repressed by Los into the Caves beneath the "dark dens of Urthona," Orc views there the splendors of the unconscious rather than its terrors; for him the unconscious is ceaseless energy. We are back in the world of the "Prolific" in *The Marriage of Heaven and Hell*, where "evil is Hell" (*MHH* plate 3). Orc is called a "Demon" and his realm, as we know from the last line of Night Five, is seen by the fallen "angel" Urizen as "hell." The symbols of the unconscious that seemed negative as the Zoas fell are positive here. Orc burns as Luvah did, but for Orc "flame Of circling fire unceasing plays to feed [his limbs] with life & bring The virtues of the Eternal worlds" (5.61.11-13). "Spirits Of life . . . dive into the deeps" (5.61.13-16), but instead of being pounded into "sea jellies" and "filaments" as Tharmas was, they "bring the thrilling joys of sense to quell [Orc's] ceaseless rage" (5.61.17). Orc does not see the "wintry," "iron" mountains known to Los, but rather the "secrets" hidden within them of "the veins of gold & silver & the hidden things of Vala" (5.61.19-20). Moreover, Orc himself is associated with the fertile element of the earth which produces its "harvest" and "vintage." He becomes what Los the blacksmith unsuccessfully tried to create on his forge:

> His knees are rocks of adamant & rubie & emerald
> Spirits of strength . . . rejoice in golden armour.
>
> (5.62.5-6)

As Blake says with his customary irony at the end of this most beautiful passage, "such is the Demon such is his terror in the nether deep" (5.62.8). This vision of the unconscious (echoed later by Orc in his Caves in 7.77.5-17) is the only passage yet in *The Four Zoas* that suggests that the formless energy of the unconscious may be something to be welcomed rather than feared. But with Urizen's approach to the Caves of Orc, the unconscious again comes to seem abhorrent. Near the end of Night Five, Urizen laments his lost consciousness (5.63.24—65.12) and then is drawn further down to the dens of Urthona by the "deep pulsations" of Orc in his Caves. But

Urizen's perception of the "Abyss" is not Orc's, and it is necessary to keep in mind their two perceptions of the same scene if one is to understand the unfolding event whose climax is the transformation of Orc into a serpent.

For Orc, "ten thousand thousand spirits Of life . . . dive into the deeps To bring the thrilling joys of sense to quell his ceaseless rage" (5.61.13-17). However Urizen's experience of the deeps as he descends at the beginning of Night Six is different: "hideous monsters of the deep annoyd him sore Scaled & finnd with iron & brass [Urizen's own metals] they devourd the path before him Incessant was the conflict" (6.69.26-28). This "conflict," which is natural to Orc as "his eyes the lights of his large soul contract or else expand" (5.61.18), frightens Urizen "& his eyes sicken at the sight" (6.69.31). The "terrors of the nether deep" which seem glorious to Orc are indeed "terrors of the Abyss" (6.70.5) to Urizen. The "forms of tygers & of Lions," the "serpents" and "worms" and "scaled monsters" (6.70.31-35) which to Orc's perception moved with an endless vitality threaten Urizen.

And when Urizen finally does approach the Caves of Orc in the beginning of Night Seven, his fearfulness makes the Caves "become what he beholds." When Urizen first sees the "Cavernd Universe of flaming fire" in which Orc is chained, the Caves are as Orc perceived them earlier in Night Five:

> . . . his lions
> Howl in the burning dens his tygers roam in the
>   redounding smoke
> . . . fierce flames
> Dance on the rivers & the rocks howling & drunk with
>   fury.
>
> (7.77.8-13)

At this point, Orc is in perfect accord with the unconscious as "howling & rending his dark caves the awful Demon lay Pulse after Pulse beat[ing] on his fetters" (7.77.20-21). But gradually, as Urizen sits "brooding . . . Age after Age," the nature of what he sees changes. The Tree of Mystery shoots up "underneath his heel" and the unconscious again begins to seem incomprehensible to human rationality and therefore something to be feared. Orc vows war on Urizen, but Urizen rejoins, "Enquire of my Sons & they shall teach thee how to War" (7.79.21); and then with terrible cynicism tells Orc the true terrors of war (7.80.9-26). Orc's perception changes and he becomes a serpent, "a Self consuming dark devourer rising into the heavens" (7.80.48). The Caves of Orc have become simply a background for the Tree of Mystery on which Orc is spread. The unconscious thus seems as ensnaring as it has to all the Zoas.

And as the Spectre of Urthona and the Shadow of Enitharmon unite underground, any last semblance of order seemingly vanishes. The Shadow and Spectre each give their confused story of the cosmogony of the Zoas, illustrating the particular errors into which Urthona-Los and Enitharmon *themselves* have fallen. According to Enitharmon, Albion mated with Vala and produced Urizen. Vala split into another Vala and Luvah, Albion in despair fell asleep, and Luvah and Urizen conspired against their father Albion. Los and Enitharmon then were born—how, Enitharmon does not know. This genealogy is contrary to Blake's own account in which the male Zoa is divided into Spectre and female Emanation. But Enitharmon's tale demonstrates the dominance of the feminine principle. Vala, who is at the center of the story, is described as the "lily of the desart" who, "melting in high noon," gave Albion "sweet bliss" as he fainted "upon her bosom" (7.83.8-9).

The Spectre finishes the cosmogony, distorting it according to Urthona-Los's own error. According to the Spectre's version, Vala was the enemy throughout. There once was an idyllic brotherhood "drinking the joys of Universal Manhood" (7.84.11), but it was destroyed by the coming of a "female bright" (7.84.16). The Spectre was the true issue born of

Enion, not Los, and the Spectre's birth shows the dominance of the masculine principle in his thinking:

> . . . I an infant terror in the womb of Enion
> My masculine spirit scorning the frail body issud forth
> From Enions brain.
>
> (7.84.23-25)

In reality, the fall of the Zoas began when Tharmas cried:

> Lost! Lost! Lost! are my Emanations . . .
> I have hidden Jerusalem in Silent Contrition
> [O Enion] I will build thee a Labyrinth also.
>
> (1.4.7-10)

The main impulse here is secrecy, as shown in Tharmas' wish to hide the Emanations "in [his] bosom" (1.4.14), and concealment generally has negative connotations in Blake's writings. "The Men have recieved their death wounds & their Emanations are fled To me for refuge" (1.4.15-16), he says, suggesting that the lost union between masculine and feminine principles is desirable, even necessary, for a "Resurrection to Unity" (1.4.4).

In the views of Shadow and Spectre, then, any balance between sexual principles is missing. The Shadow of Enitharmon loses all human semblance as she runs "raving about the upper Elements in maddning fury" (7.85.12). She gives birth to an unnatural "wonder horrible" (7.85.17), who is yet another manifestation of "howling Orc." The birth is accompanied by death, not life, as "many of the dead burst forth from the bottoms of their tombs" (7.85.18) in a grotesque parody of the Last Judgment. Form and order of any kind disappear.

By this point in the poem, all of the Zoas have fallen into their own versions of the unconscious. As they faced archetypes of the unconscious, they either succumbed to the chaos implicit in these archetypes or, rejecting it in fear, they tried to build some rigid construct that would protect them against "Utmost

Extinction." It will be remembered that these are the two neurotic reactions to the unconscious that Jung outlines.

The two Zoas who are closest to the unconscious by their natures—Luvah, Zoa of passion, and Tharmas, Zoa of Sensation—follow the former course. Luvah remains in his furnaces until he is let out as "molten metal" to be recast and reformed by the Sons of Urizen, thus losing his original shape. Tharmas as "God of the Waters" "depart[s] far into the Unknown" (4.52.8) in Night Four, becoming one with the unconscious with all individual identity lost. Thereafter in the poem he acts as Poseidon, who also inhabited the watery depths with silence and power.

The other two Zoas follow the second course as they confront formlessness and desperately try to construct some refuge that has firm boundaries and a systematic organization. The protection of these constructions is never ultimately successful. Thus in the beginning of Night One, when Albion falls into his sleep, Urizen "pale . . . [beholds] the Abyss" around which wanders "blind Enion,"and "mighty was the draught of Voidness to draw Existence in" (2.23.15—24.1). Terrified, the Urizen who had originally risen "like a star . . . exulting" (2.23.9-10), now sees "the indefinite space beneath" the sleeping Albion, and "his soul [shrinks] with horror His feet upon the verge of Non Existence" (2.24.3-4). Hurriedly, he builds the Mundane Shell with "compasses, the quadrant & the rule & balance," as well as the furnaces into which Luvah is soon cast. And so Urizen does not create the order he had anticipated after all, for "in woe & fear he [sees] Vala incircle round the furnaces where Luvah was clos'd" (2.25.44—26.1).

Los confronts "non-Entity" in Night Four, when Tharmas "rapes Enitharmon away" with him into "the Abyss." Los's ensuing experience is the same as Urizen's has been:

Terrified Los beheld the ruins of Urizen beneath
A horrible Chaos to his eyes. a formless unmeasurable Death
. . .
Then Los with terrible hands siezd on the Ruind Furnaces

Of Urizen. Enormous work: he builded them anew
Labour of Ages in the Darkness . . .

(4.52.11-17)

So Los builds the fallen world of the senses, creating Time and
Space as he gives Urizen form. Los's reaction to his finished
creation was Urizen's earlier reaction:

In terrors Los shrunk from his task . . .
Pale terror siezd the Eyes of Los as he beat round
The hurtling Demon. terrifid at the shapes
Enslavd humanity put on he became what he beheld
He became what he was doing he was himself transformed.

(4.55.16-23)

The fallen world is as limited a protection against "Chaos" as
was the Mundane Shell.

In Night Six, Urizen falls beneath the world of Generation
which Los has created "into the dismal void . . . Whirling in
unresistible revolutions" (6.71.21-22). All sense of inner bal-
ance lost, Urizen falls onto a bed of "slime" which appears to
be the last limit before this "dismal void," and here again he
creates an organized structure: Ulro. He declares himself
"King" of this realm, but it is an empty declaration, as he dis-
covers in the next Night, when he confronts Orc in his Caves.
And as Urizen builds Ulro against the "Abyss of Night" in
Night Six, so his Tree of Mystery becomes at the end of Night
Seven "a Shelter from the tempests of Void" (7.84.2) for the
Spectre of Urthona and the Shadow of Enitharmon. But it is as
useless a shelter as was Ulro.

Yet Regeneration does begin, when all seems utterly lost.
For as Los and Enitharmon build Golgonooza together near the
end of Night Seven, they assume the third approach to the un-
conscious that Jung discusses. This Golgonooza is the first *hu-
manly* created mandala in the poem, made because Los is finally
able to feel Christ's own reaction to the "Human polypus of
death" in Night Five. Blake deliberately connects this creation
with his own art: Los and Enitharmon "draw" and "tincture"

exactly like William and Catherine. For Blake here the artistic imagination works as Jung says the psyche works, forcing the artist to understand and order *both* sides of human nature: the "Prolific" and the "Devourer," the myth and the non-myth. Artistic creation in *The Four Zoas* thus assumes the same spiritual significance as the mandala. As Blake himself says, "Jesus & his Apostles & Disciples were all Artists."[21]

None of the Zoas or Emanations previously acted as Los and Enitharmon do in these pages. This first actualization by Blake of the "Regeneration by the Resurrection from the dead" (1.4.5) is an apprehension of psychological unity. Los adjures Enitharmon not to seek Christ "on the outside of Existence but look! behold! take comfort! Turn inwardly thine Eyes & there behold the Lamb of God" (7.87.44-45). The actions of Zoa and Emanation seem Christlike. Golgonooza becomes a true mandala, its creators having internalized the "Divine Vision"—and artistic creation thus performs Christ's function.

Los's building of Golgonooza clearly parallels Urizen's construction of the Mundane Shell in Night Two, but Los's mandala is successful, as Urizen's was not. The order that Urizen was seeking was external and inhuman, one-sidedly rationalistic. This "Architect divine" attempted the ridiculous feat of squaring the heavens by a line (2.30.10) as he "measure[d] out the course of heaven" (2.28.21) and built in the "deeps" of the "vast unknown." The order which Los seeks is internal:

[He] Builded Golgonooza Los labouring builded pillars high
And Domes terrific in the nether heavens for beneath
Was opend new heavens & a new Earth beneath & within
Threefold within the brain within the heart within the
    loins.

(7.87.7-10)

Los's mandala is thus located in man's psychological depths as he builds in "the nether heavens" and finds a "new Earth" for

[21] *P & P,* p. 271.

his art "within." At the center of Urizen's mandala was the Druidical and slavishly obedient Ahania, his "Shadowy Feminine Semblance" (2.30.23), a perversion of the Anthropos. By contrast, the *hieros gamos* is at least potentially at the heart of Golgonooza as Los and Enitharmon finally begin to work together. The mandala desired by the Daughters of Beulah on page 20 begins to be realized as Los's Golgonooza "opens . . . within the heart within the loins."

Yet this mandala is still an incomplete one, still merely a protective device against the threatening chaos. Enitharmon here understands the possible effects of that "Eternal Death" as she never has before, certainly as she never did in her Song on page 34 in Night Two which celebrated destruction. She eats the Edenic fruit from Urizen's Tree of Mystery and gives it to Los as well, an action that seems consistent with the ferocious jealousy of that earlier page 34 ("The joy of woman is the Death of her most best beloved"—2.34.63) but is not. Here she follows what she fearfully perceives to be the law of life ("Life lives upon Death & by devouring appetite All things subsist on one another"—7.87.19-20). Los also eats the fruit. The two wait for Christ and "life eternal," hoping for order *while in* chaos. One should remember the previous reactions of Zoas and Emanations to this same feared polarity: either a complete loss of conscious identity, or an attempted imposition of order for the sake of order.

Jung has written that "since man knows himself only as an ego, and the self . . . is indistinguishable from a God-image, *self-realization . . . amounts to God's incarnation*" [italics added].[22] Here, Los and Enitharmon come to share Christ's insight when he faced the formlessness of the polypus that "in every human bosom these limits stand." Gradually the Zoa and Emanation acknowledge a psychological correspondence to the external chaos that they see about them. Los forgives Enitharmon's "ancient injuries" of "jealousy & fear & terror" and says, "I also tremble at myself & at all my former life"

[22] Jung, *Psychology and Religion*, p. 157.

(7.87.48-52). Enitharmon too sees that what she fears is an inward, not an outward state, as she laments that "Eternal Death" is

> Uttermost extinction . . .
> An ever dying life of stifling & obstruction shut out
> Of existence to be a sign & terror to all who behold
> Lest any should in futurity do as we have done . . .
> Such is our state . . .
>
> > (7.87.56-60)

Los himself begins to assume Christ's "mild and gentle" mien of that earlier passage as the Zoa calls on his Emanation to sacrifice her Selfhood by giving herself up to "Extinction" and "Eternal Death" so as to comfort the "Spectrous Dead":

> Thy bosom translucent is a soft repose for the weeping souls
> Of those piteous victims of battle there they sleep in happy
> > obscurity
> They feed upon our life we are their victims.
>
> > (7.90.6-8)

His desire to develop Golgonooza further is couched in words Christ might use:

> . . . stern desire
> I feel to fabricate embodied semblances in which the dead
> May live before us in our palaces & in our gardens of labour
> > . . .
> To form a world of Sacrifice . . .
>
> > (7.90.8-12)

Enitharmon acquiesces and encourages him to work on Golgonooza, but a Golgonooza with a religious as well as artistic purpose: to "fabricate forms sublime . . . [that] They shall be ransoms for our Souls that we may live" (7.90.22-24). Christ has thus truly acted as an archetype of the Self for Los (who sets to work at once, "his hands divine inspired"), showing him by example how to construct a "city of art," which, paradoxically, will have as its essential ingredient all that it originally had been built to repulse.

It is instructive to compare Los's earlier building of Golgonooza in Night Five with his construction of it here, for pages 87 and 90 show a relationship between art and Blake's myth that is new. When Orc is born in Night Five,

> Los [around Enitharmon] builded pillars of iron
> And brass & silver & gold fourfold in dark prophetic fear
>
> . . .
>
> Tharmas laid the Foundations & Los finishd it in howling woe.
>
> (5.59.28—60.5)

The rigidity with which Golgonooza is created suggests the rigidity of its purpose: exclusion of Orc and the elements of Los's unconscious that he represents. Golgonooza is like a prison around Enitharmon (although that does not prevent the "family romance" from developing), created out of a fear of the unconscious, which the other Zoas also have experienced at this point in *The Four Zoas*. Their elements of brass, iron, silver, and gold are its pillars, and Tharmas, "parent power," lays the foundations.

But Los's "fabricat[ion] of forms divine" in Night Seven is utterly different. It is worth quoting this passage in full, for if we consider it together with Nights Eight and Nine, we can see a mythos developing that imaginatively contains what it before attempted merely to transcend:

> . . . Los his hands divine inspired began
> To modulate his fires studious the loud roaring flames
> He vanquishd with the strength of Art bending their iron points
> And drawing them forth delighted upon the winds of Golgonooza
> From out the ranks of Urizens war & from the fiery lake
> Of Orc bending down as the binder of the Sheaves follows

> The reaper in both arms embracing the furious raging
> flames
> Los drew them forth out of the deeps planting his right foot
> firm
> Upon the Iron crag of Urizen thence springing up aloft
> Into the heavens of Enitharmon in a mighty circle.
>
> (7.90.25-34)

The incomplete mandala is thus completed and the *hieros gamos* realized, for, as we see in lines immediately following, this "mighty circle" is "tinctured" by Enitharmon and "divided into just proportions" by Los. The two are roused from their despair as regenerated artists. The imagery of the quoted passage confirms Jung's point that a true mandala, "itself a source of energy," arises from the centers of energy in the psyche. The "furious flames . . . out of the deeps" recalls Orc's "Cavernd Universe of flaming fire" (7.77.6), where "a flame Of circling fire unceasing play[ed]" (5.61.11-12) over Orc's chained limbs, an intentional echo, since Los draws these flames "from out the ranks of Urizens war [Urizen at this point is in the Caves of Orc] & from the fiery lake Of Orc." Here Los is creating Golgonooza out of the very stuff that was earlier the source of so much anguish for him: the "malignant fires" of Orc that had motivated Los's "Chain of Jealousy."

His earlier states of mind as he tried to create order show why his present effort in Night Seven, by contrast, is finally successful. In Night Four, when he made Urizen's sensuous body, he strove to conquer and transform the materials used, with his "blows" on "the Anvils of Iron . . . petrify[ing] with incessant beating many a rock. many a planet" (4.52.18-19) and "his pity secret feeding on thoughts of cruelty" (4.53.14). In Night Five, after Orc was born, Los created Golgonooza in a state of incoherent dissociation, "mourn[ing] in anguish fierce Coverd with gloom" (5.59.26-27) and finishing his structure "in howling woe" (5.60.5). Both passages show a confused separation between the artist and his creation.

But in Night Seven, Los strives with his materials with a vigor and joy born of a unified vision. He has here a conscious, imaginative grasp of these flames which is new for him, and surpasses Orc's abandoned merging into similar flames earlier in Night Seven (Orc lay in them, "pulse after pulse beat[ing] on his fetters"—7.77.21). Los "modulates" these flames, drawing them out "delighted upon the winds of Golgonooza," and thus incorporates them into the mandala with their form-less energy channeled but still present. Los, more now than the blacksmith of Blake's earlier metaphor, is identified with the artist who "vanquish[ed] with the strength of Art." In an an-ticipation of the agricultural imagery of Night Nine, Los is the "binder of the Sheaves" who "in both arms embrac[es] the furious raging flames," no longer fearing them but using them as an essential source of energy for Golgonooza. He "plant[s] his right foot firm," suggesting Blake's position in his garden at the end of *Milton*. Here as there, it is implied that the artist is finally able to assume the bard's poetic stance; more, Los here is also asserting his powers of consciousness in the face of unconscious contents.

The passage that concludes this page makes this assertion clearer still. Here Enitharmon gives birth to Rintrah and Palamabron, sons very much in Orc's mold. Seeing them, "Orc was comforted in the deeps his soul revivd in them" (7.90.46). Before, Los had built Golgonooza as a refuge against the threat of "Extinction" which his sons seemed to pose; now he "rather [chooses] to meet Eternal death than to destroy The offspring of their Care & Pity" (7.90.52-53). Los seems Christlike as he sacrifices himself for others.

Not only does Los accept his children, he also accepts his old enemy Urizen, no longer fearing the bondage of this Zoa who in Night One declared himself "God from Eternity to Eter-nity" (1.12.8). Nor does he fear the "horrible Chaos" and "formless unmeasurable Death" caused by this same Urizen's fall in Night Four. And as Los perceives Urizen with "love & not hate" (7.90.65), Urizen amazingly then assumes the form

of one of Los's own sons ("an infant Lovely breathd from
Enitharmon"—7.90.66-67). In these lines that conclude
Night Seven, Los no longer sees Urizen as the patriarchal
"Ancient of Days":

> [Los's] whole soul loved him he beheld him an infant
> Lovely breathd from Enitharmon he trembled within
>   himself.

(7.90.66-67)

Los is as "mild and gentle" towards Urizen as Jesus was to-
ward the "Human Polypus," and the old "Architect Divine"
whom Blake has castigated so many times and in so many
guises begins to "rise again" as Christ predicted, literally re-
born in these lines. The Zoas exist here as living beings with-
out their stereotyped mythic characteristics that Blake had
given them in poem after poem: Urizen's predilection for
measuring, systematizing, trying to impose one Law and one
Religion; Los's persistent howling, building among his fur-
nace, beating with "the thundering Hammer of Urthona"
(4.52.28-29). Here, the essential quality of the Zoas is
nakedness—nakedness of Urizen's form as newborn "infant,"
nakedness of feeling in Los who "trembled within himself."
Each Zoa becomes the conscious relative of the other, and the
Christlike Los finds Urizen "now In his hands" (7.90.64-65).

Night Eight changes the *nature* of the apocalypse as con-
ceived by Blake, and the eschatological "Regeneration" that
comes in Night Nine shows a regeneration of Blake's mythos
as well. Superficially, the narrative of Night Eight follows the
traditions of eschatological literature that predict the coming
of the Antichrist and his final struggle with Christ before the
earth is purged of evil in the apocalypse. Certainly the plot of
The Four Zoas requires Christ and Antichrist to face each other
in this last battle before the end of time, and Blake would have
had to devote this last Night before the apocalypse to these
two dominant figures. But closer examination of the Night
shows that Blake's treatment of the Antichrist is decidedly un-

Blake in Night Eight is beginning to bring together an-
tinomies, rendering the archetypal power of the one previously
feared polarity.

Night Eight opens rather quietly with a protective mandala
formed by Albion and two angels sent by the Council of God:

> Two winged immortal shapes one standing at his feet
> Toward the East one standing at his head toward the west
> Their wings joind in the Zenith over head.
>
> (8.99.7-9)

Jung says of the triadic mandala that it is "much rarer" than
tetradic figures, and "should be regarded as [a] 'disturbed' to-
tality picture."[26] Here Albion is still in his "Sleep of Death,"
still sunk in unconsciousness. He wakes, but not to action as
he "repos[es] In the saviours arms, in the arms of tender mercy
& loving kindness" (8.99.13-14). Los and Enitharmon also see
Christ without much more enthusiasm as "wondring with love
& Awe they felt the divine hand upon them" (8.99.18). As
they worship peacefully, the inhabitants of Beulah see the
"Divine Vision." Enitharmon goes on weaving her feminine
extension of Golgonooza that she had begun at the end of
Night Seven, the mandala which will prove a battlement
against the forces of Satan. And those forces immediately
begin to mobilize.

But when we pass to Blake's account of "Orc a Serpent form
augmenting times on times," we see an energy missing in
those previous pages. Orc seems to grow into the familiar dra-
gon which appears in nearly all traditional accounts of the An-
tichrist. But there is definite ambiguity in Blake's description
of him, for Orc is covered with "scales of pearl then gold &
silver" and "down his back & bosom The Emerald Onyx Sap-
phire jasper beryl amethyst Strove in terrific emulation which
should gain a place Upon the mighty Fiend" (8.101.10-16).
Surely it is not a coincidence that these are the very gems
which John says are the materials of the New Jerusalem in *Rev-*

26 Jung, *Archetypes*, pp. 361-62.

traditional, being closer to Jung's conception of the Antichrist
as an aspect of the archetype of Self, which must be included in
the total vision, than to John's portrayal of "that old serpent
. . . Satan" that must be cast out at the end.

Indeed, Jung holds that Lucifer is the elder son of God and
Christ is the younger. Christ as the gloriously unspotted figure
seems one-sided to Jung, lacking real wholeness, since the
dark side of existence is specifically omitted by being concen-
trated on the figure of Satan. Jung sees Satan as having strong
psychological ties with the unconscious, "the archetype . . .
appear[ing] from behind in its 'wrathful' form, as the 'dark son
of chaos.' "[23] The Antichrist thus is as much a manifestation
of the Self as is Christ, complementing the bright figure of
Christ with his darkness. The coming of the Antichrist is seen
as an inexorable psychological law implying *enantiodromia*.[24]

This proves to be close to Blake's final vision in Nights
Eight and Nine. Christ's relation to chaos and the "dark
opake" Satan grows more and more intimate, and Blake's cen-
sure of the Antichrist more and more ambiguous as *The Four
Zoas* progresses. Urizen assumes the dread serpentine charac-
teristics of the Antichrist during the poem, yet he is embraced
by Los at the end of Night Seven. Night Eight gives us a grow-
ing *acceptance* of the Antichrist and the "portions of eternity"
which he represents. As we shall see in Night Nine, he is re-
ally one more agent of the Lord in the apocalypse.

The general psychological movement of Night Eight is suc-
cinctly if technically described by Jung in his analysis of the
Antichrist as a variation on the archetype of the Self: "Every
intensified differentiation of the Christ-image brings about a
corresponding accentuation of its unconscious complement,
thereby increasing the tension between above and below."[25]
When Christ appears in Night Eight, so does the Antichrist,
as if called forth by him. The Satan first appearing as the dis-
tant Other who is "Abominable deadly" and "dark opake" be-

23 *Ibid.*, p. 117.   24 Jung, *Aion*, p. 43.
25 *Ibid.*

comes truly awesome by the end of the Night in his "wrath & majesty."

Christ opens and closes the Night. He is part of the Council of God that watches Albion in the beginning, and he is the dominant figure in Enion's vision at the conclusion. But within this "frame" the Antichrist emerges as a polarity of existence in his own right. He first appears as:

> . . . a Shadowy hermaphrodite black & opake
> The Soldiers namd it Satan but he was yet unformd & vast
> Hermaphroditic it at length became hiding the Male
> Within as in a Tabernacle Abominable Deadly.
>
> (8.101.34-37)

His hermaphroditic nature is further stressed a few pages later, as well as his alliance with Vala:

> . . . at length an awful wonder burst
> From the Hermaphroditic bosom Satan he was namd
> Son of Perdition terrible his form dishumanizd monstrous
> A male without a female counterpart . . .
> Yet hiding the shadowy female Vala as in an ark & Curtains.
>
> (8.104.22-27)

Blake's characterization of Vala in religious terms ("as in an ark & Curtains") has several meanings. She is the false church of *Revelation*; within Blake's own myth she also represents institutionalized religion swathed in concealing curtains reminiscent of Urizen's Net of Religion. Further, she reinforces Blake's conception of Satan as hermaphroditic. One cannot help recalling the many androgynous cosmogonic gods in world religions (as in Indian and Egyptian mythologies). Traditionally, such hermaphroditism symbolizes perfection and eternal unity because it is beyond the human. For Blake, the figure of the hermaphrodite is symbolic of chaos and utter *imperfection* precisely because it is beyond the human. The forces that fight by Satan's side are similarly characterized as hermaphroditic. They are "monsters of the Elements Lions or Ty-

gers or Wolves" (8.102.3) who briefly assume a human form because of Los's hammering and Enitharmon's singing, but then return to their original chaotic forms. Blake says of the war, "it took a hideous form Seen in the aggregate a Vast Hermaphroditic form" (8.104.19-20). For Blake, there is an inherent horror in this conception of the Antichrist: he calls Satan "dishumanized monstrous."

However, this "as yet unformed & vast" figure of Satan has a gathering power that suggests it is a force in its own right, issuing from that "Voidness" which in Night Two had threatened "to draw Existence in" (2.24.1). It is similar to the Contrary of the "Devourer," which is not merely the absence of good nor the instrument of God. It exists in itself, not dualistically but as one antimony of existence which is necessary for that existence. When Satan appears in Night Eight, Los is inspired to action more vigorous than the quiet worship of the opening pages. Now he is building "the Walls of Golgonooza against the stirring battle" with the passion shown on page 90 of Night Seven. One opposite calls forth the other: Satan comes "abominable Deadly" and the "Holy Spirit . . . inspir[es] . . . Enormous Works" of Los.

Furthermore, the poetic quality of the Night as a whole is uneven, which tells us something about where Blake's true sympathies as artist lay. Generally, the sections in which the Antichrist emerges have a vitality lacking in the pages showing the converted Los and Enitharmon, the "sons of Eden," and the "Lamb of God." This latter group of pages seems to have primarily an expository purpose, with the characters rather passively declaring what has happened, what is happening, and to whom it is happening. Perhaps there simply is not much variety possible in the description of salvation, but words such as "wondring," "ecstasy," "astonishd," and "rapturous" occur with a certain predictability. This may seem like an ironic fulfillment of Blake's famous statement that "Milto[n] wrote in fetters when he wrote of Angels & God, and at libert[y] when of Devils & Hell" (*MHH* 5), but I think rather th[at]

elation 21:11-21. There is thus more than a suggestion that the Antichrist may have a place in the overall pattern after all. In Orc's "fury" and "writhing contortive" there is a vigor unmatched in the earlier accounts of Los feeling "the Divine hand . . . upon him," Enitharmon "singing lulling cadences" and "sighing forth . . . Lamentations," and Albion "repos[ing] in the saviours arms."

And indeed the Antichrist proves to be a "manifestation . . . of [the] dark aspect . . . of the self,"[27] as we see when Armageddon finally does begin. Urizen acts as he had in Night Seven before Los embraced him, his behavior issuing out of a "mighty rage" that causes "sparkles of Dire affliction" to "issu[e] round his frozen limbs." His furious activity parallels Orc's as he "twists," "bores," and "rams" his "warlike preparations," and in a variation of his creation of the Net of Religion he again tries to constrain through "hooks & nets" and "cords of iron and brass." Urizen uses the explosives of modern warfare in this eschatological battle, "molten metals cast in hollow globes & . . . tubes in petrific steel & . . . combustibles & wheels And chains & pullies" (8.100.26-31). The effect is to make the horror pungent and immediate, creating an energetic involvement of response. We suddenly see that this Armageddon is not waged between angels and demons, with the angels "pour[ing] out the vials of the wrath of God upon the earth" (*Rev.* 16:1). Rather, man is hastening *himself* toward the final destruction. It will come as a result of man's own psychology, whose manifestations are as terrible as anything envisioned by John of Patmos.

Yet as this polarity seems dominant, the other begins to move toward ascendancy again. The "shadowy female Vala" whom Urizen has enshrined within, and who has seemed unrelievedly treacherous throughout the poem, acts as his Emanation as she reminds him of the wisdom that Ahania had spoken long ago in Night Three: Vala mourns for Luvah and declares the uselessness of power without love. Vala (even Vala!) appar-

[27] Jung, *Aion*, p. 44.

ently is redeemable, for she hints at the necessity of Christ's coming:

> But happiness can never [come] to thee O King nor me
> For [Luvah] was source of every joy that this mysterious
> tree
> Unfolds in Allegoric fruit. When shall the dead revive
> Can that which has existed cease or can love & life Expire.
>
> (8.103.17-20)

The result of Vala's speech is essentially the same as the result of Ahania's in Night Three: Urizen's fall from eminence. His Net of Religion collapses, tangling "himself . . . in his own net in sorrow lust repentance" (8.103.31), and Urizen disappears until he assumes the final guise of the Antichrist pages later.

The Sons of Eden sing more explicitly than Vala of the coming of "the Lamb of God," though the body of their Song on page 113 seems more statement than paean. The Sons themselves on that page seem to be passive witnesses rather than active participants as they describe the activities of "Enitharmons Looms & Los's Forges And the Spindles of Tirzah & Rahab and the Mills of Satan & Beelzeboul" (8.113.1-2). Forges, looms, and mills all work simultaneously, clothing and unclothing the "weeping spectres of the dead" continually. For the sake of narrative clarity, Erdman follows Blake's instructions in the manuscript to insert this page of exposition into the middle of page 104, the page on which the Sons begin their Song. But if we read the first and second portions of page 104 together, a fact emerges whose thematic importance is somewhat dissipated by Blake's final arrangement. In the opening seventeen lines of page 104, the Sons of Eden descant upon the "Lamb of God," envisioning the *collapse* of distinctions between Christ and Antichrist:

> Glory Glory Glory to the holy Lamb of God
> Who now beginneth to put off the dark Satanic body . . .
> . . . we now behold

> Where Death Eternal is put off Eternally
> Assume the dark Satanic body in the Virgins womb
> O Lamb divin[e] . . . Come then O Lamb of God
> Come Lord Jesus come quickly.
>
> (8.104.6-17)

And what comes immediately is the "hermaphroditic" Satan, the Females of Amalek, and Urizen as Antichrist.

The "dark aspect of the Self" is rendered by the Females of Amalek even more vividly than by Urizen among his war machines, for whereas Urizen merely created the instruments of destruction, the Females use them with a terrible relish. Their hypocritical concern for their victims whom they torture is somehow much worse than Urizen's frank glorying in human suffering. Rebellion seems impossible from creatures who are able to sing:

> Go Noah fetch the girdle of strong brass heat it red hot
> Press it around the loins of this expanding cruelty
> Shriek not so my only love . . .
>
> (8.105.44-46)

Interwoven into this Song are sexual hypocrisy (the "torments of love & jealousy" inevitably experienced "in the Death and Judgment of Albion the Ancient Man," as Blake suggests in the title to the entire poem), specific tortures of medieval religious persecutions (the "hot iron," the heated "brass girdle," the "screw of iron" with which to pierce tongue and ears), and practices common to industrial mills ("my soul is seven furnaces incessant roars the bellows Upon my terribly flaming heart the molten metal runs In channels thro my fiery limbs"—8.105.38-40). It might seem that the Females are simply singing as one would expect representatives of the "Female Will" to sing, trying to constrain the male to the world of Generation ("our life depends on this . . . [that] my beloved is bound upon the Stems of Vegetation"—8.105.51-53). The horror goes immeasurably deeper than that, however, for Blake seems to be saying that this side of human behavior is not to be explained away; nor will it disappear as easily as his earlier enthusiastic proclamation suggested when the apocalypse dawned at the end of *The Marriage of Heaven and Hell*: "Empire is no more! and now the lion & wolf shall cease."

Following this wild maenadic song is Los's list of his generations to Rahab, which seems tame by contrast. His analysis to her of the "State named Satan" seems like a lecture, and his naming of the Seven Eyes of God not a particularly effective way to persuade this mother of the Females of Amalek to worship the Christ upon whom she has just experienced the transports of sadism. It is no wonder that "Rahab burning with pride & revenge departed from Los" (8.116.3).

As Blake revised his manuscript and separated portions of page 104 with a page of exposition whose place in the action is best understood by this arrangement, so he separated page 106. Here, however, the first portion seems to have been distinct in Blake's own mind also, since he wrote it sideways in the margin. But there is the same resulting sacrifice of emphasis here as on page 104. Page 106 begins with Christ's followers mourning his crucifixion and, in effect, echoing the sons of Eden who had cried, "Come Lord Jesus come quickly." And as on page 104, the Antichrist appears in response, rather than the "Lamb of God."

Urizen experiences on pages 106 and 107 what Orc had experienced when he was transformed, but we enter into that experience with Urizen, as we did not with Orc. In Night Seven Orc begins "to Organize a Serpent body . . . A Self consuming dark devourer rising into the heavens" (7.80.44-48); near the opening of Night Eight he is a "Serpent . . . augmenting times on times" (8.101.5). Blake reports this event, but he does not realize it, so that "the Spectator [may] Enter into these Images in his Imagination approaching them on the Fiery Chariot of his Contemplative Thought."[28] Urizen's assumption of the guise of the Antichrist, however, is rendered with a vitality

[28] *P & P*, p. 550.

unmatched by any previous passage in the Night describing either Christ or Antichrist. "Evil is the active springing from Energy," Blake wrote fifteen to twenty years earlier in *The Marriage of Heaven and Hell* (plate 3), and the "evil" portrayed here is not so very different in spirit from the "evil" of that earlier work, although Blake's portrayal of that polarity has passed beyond the irony of *The Marriage of Heaven and Hell.*

At first "a dull & numming stupor" overcomes Urizen, and he sits "Stonied upon his rock" (exactly as will the Zoas when they too are faced with the Antichrist archetype). However, as his outward form becomes "that old serpent . . . Satan," he regains the strength of motion and the terrible energy of the archetype. He is no longer Urizen, Zoa and "faculty" of Albion, but is "abominable to the eyes of mortals" (8.106.33). He is possessed by an alien power as "his mouth wide opening tongueless His teeth a triple row . . . And his immense tail lashd the Abyss" (8.106.29-31). The "light" hitherto associated with Urizen has signified rationality and consciousness, the basic attribute of the masculine and powerful sun god. Here, Blake enlarges the significance of that quality to include the other more chthonic associations of that "light" which emanates from fire, destroying yet purifying in its burning heat. Orc knew this aspect of "light" in his Caves as "crackling the flames went up with fury from the immortal demon" and "surrounded with flames the Demon grew loud howling in his fires" (5.61.5-6). And so does Urizen, as "the King of Light outstretched in fury,"

> . . . his Eyelids like the Sun
> Arising in his pride enlighten all the Grizly deeps
> His scales transparent give forth light like windows of the
>   morning
> His neck flames with wrath & majesty.

(8.106.42-45)

Those parts of the natural world that had formed the Zoa's deadening construct of Ulro here are animated and revitalized as the possessed Urizen

> . . . lashes the Abyss
> Beating the Desarts & the rocks the desarts feel his power
> They shake their slumbers off. They wave in awful fear.
>
> (8.106.45-47)

Those creatures which Urizen had faced with trepidation in Night Six as he approached the Caves of Orc (the lion, the tiger, and the horse) are here as affected by Urizen as are "the desarts & the rocks," no longer feared by him. In Blake's poetry, these animals always are associated with unconscious, uncontrollable energy. They will be reanimated in Night Nine, when the apocalypse begins and Christ comes; now as the Antichrist comes, "they view the light & wonder crying out in terrible existence" (8.107.7).

The last sight that we have of Urizen as Antichrist is one of vigorous struggle and movement, "ruthfulness" and "fury." At this point Orc (who is similarly possessed by the archetype) merges with Urizen, and this dark aspect of the archetype threatens dominance with its "indefinite lust." The effect upon the other Zoas is the effect that the unconscious has upon the overwhelmed ego: loss of any conscious identity at all as they whirl about in a "stony stupor." Interestingly, the fate of Los and Enitharmon as they experience this is described with a different metaphor—*the loss of outline*—as:

> . . . the vessels of [Los's] blood
> Dart forth upon the wind in pipes writhing about in the
>   Abyss . . .
> Into a form of Vegetation living . . .
> Moving in rootlike fibres trembling in fear upon the Earth.
>
> (8.107.26-30)

Fittingly, those Emanations who have before been given such powerful insights into the unconscious in their chants are the only ones here to keep their identities as Orc and Urizen, now agents of the unconscious, "reign over all." Ahania again chants a "vision of dark futurity," a vision of Albion "the Eternal Man" as he exists in the realm of the Antichrist (appropriately, since it is her Zoa who has taken the form of the Antichrist). Her chant is balanced by Enion's vision of Man as he will appear in the domain of Christ. Christ and Antichrist as aspects of the archetype of Self are thus reunited in this conclusion to Night Eight, both catalyzing the process of Individuation by which Albion's "Regeneration by the Resurrection from the dead" will be realized.

Ahania says that her vision is of "universal death"; however, it is not really death that she sees, but the reality of "the dark body of corruptible death" and the endless way in which life (however lowly and seemingly loathsome) issues forth from it. On the surface, it might seem that her vision is a despairing picture of "universal death devour[ing] all," but Blake gives us this vision with the same ambiguity that he has given us the Antichrist. Ahania cries of the dying lion and horse, majestic and sympathetic animals, but as she does so she also cries of the ignoble creatures that come to life out of them: the worms that in the belly of the dead lion "feast on his death," the "serpents devouring one another," which will also devour the horse that "seeks for the [serpents'] pool to lie him down & die" (8.109.7-10). Albion too, who seems without life as he "sleeps in the Earth nor feels the vigrous sun Nor silent moon" and "round [whose] limbs the Serpent Orc Fold without fold encompasses" (8.108.23-26), is part of that process. He lies on his rock "marrowless bloodless," his eyes sunk in his skull and his flesh shrunk on his bones. Yet his "corrupting" body supports life: the "Scaly monsters of the restless deep" that "annoy the nether parts," the weeds that wrap his head, the slime that covers his flesh. Above him circles a "famishd" eagle.

Contrapuntally, Enion answers Ahania by chanting of Christ's coming and of what Man will be like after that coming. In both the beginning and the conclusion of the Night, then, the "Divine Vision" is perceived *while in* chaos and death. The inhabitants of Beulah thus

. . . saw the Saviour beyond the Pit of death & destruction
For whether they lookd upward they saw the Divine Vision

> Or whether they lookd downward still they saw the Divine
>   Vision
> Surrounding them on all sides beyond sin & death & hell.
>
>   (8.100.13-16)

So too Enion chants to Ahania of "the Lamb of God's return" while she is in "the Caverns of the Grave." This is a great advance psychologically in the poem, since before the Zoas and Emanations could not conceive of order and chaos together without one predominating over the other, either order swamped by chaos or chaos rigidly "controlled" by order.

The prelude to Enion's vision on page 108 is similar to Ahania's in that it is concerned with decay, but the emphasis shifts, for Enion sings of her own oncoming decay ("the Earthworm came in dismal state I found him in my bosom") which she sees as one step in the process of "Regeneration." She completes Ahania's portrayal of "the dark body of corruptible death" as she says, "Listen I will tell thee what is done in the caverns of the grave" (8.109.35). Her first words on page 110 are of "the Lamb of God . . . soon to return," but the body of her chant describes a Christlike "Man" who is "collecting up the scatterd portions of his immortal body" (8.110.7). Albion here functions both as a character in the context of the poem who comprehends man's pain and suffering, and as a vision by Blake of the body politic finally cognizant of the social chaos all around it. He plows his fields, harvests his grain, and stores it in his granary, knowing that these "elemental forms of everything that grows" will ultimately be resurrected as he will when the "Lamb of God" returns. There is a suggestion that the Zoas will act in this "Resurrection," for Blake specifies that Albion performs his duties in each of the directions associated with the Zoas:

> He tries the sullen north wind riding on its angry furrows
> The sultry south when the sun rises & the angry east
> When the sun sets . . .
> . . . And in the gentle West
> Reposes where the Suns heat dwells.
>
>   (8.110.9-15)

As Albion has gathered the "Elemental forms" of "tree & herb
& fish & bird & beast," so he also sees that man "Labour[s] &
sorrow[s] & learn[s] & forget[s] & return[s] To the dark valley
whence he came to begin his labours anew In pain he sighs in
pain he labours" (8.110.19-21)—man waiting as Albion is
waiting "till [the Eternal Man] reassumes his ancient bliss"
(8.110.28). Albion also is a figure who is returned to his pre-
industrial days, and who mourns over his sons of present-day
England still suffering war and famine:

> . . . [Man] labours in his universe
> Screaming in birds over the deep & howling in the Wolf
> Over the slain & moaning in the cattle & in the winds.
>   (8.110.21-23)

Blake would seem to be saying that Albion himself will be-
come Christlike in the apocalypse. Blake uses the familiar
symbol of Christ as husbandman to suggest this, and this
prophecy of man becoming Christlike may not seem like a very
surprising one for Blake to make. But this anticipates the cen-
tral metaphor of Night Nine—the Zoas who as husbandmen
plow, winnow, and harvest mankind—and predicts the ac-
tions of that coming Night (even the "pain" and "sorrow" that
the "Human Harvest" will endure). This passage should be
considered in conjunction with 9.138.27-35, which repeats
the metaphor and ideas of Enion's chants almost exactly. Here
the newly regenerated Albion rises:

> Calling the Plowman to his Labour & the Shepherd to his
>   rest . . .
> Conversing with the Animal forms of wisdom night & day
> For Tharmas brought his flocks upon the hills & in the Vales
>
>   . . .
> Among the wooly flock The hammer of Urthona sounds.
>   (9.138.29-35)

The Zoas here have become something more than mere
scourges of God, and Albion is at once psychologically and
politically "regenerated," finally returned as he is to that "an-
cient time" when "the holy Lamb of God" was "on Englands

pleasant pastures seen." It is hard to overemphasize the importance of Nights Eight and Nine. With the emergence of the Antichrist as a powerfully energetic (almost beautiful) figure in Night Eight, Ahania's and Enion's affirmation of life "from the Caverns of the Grave," and Enion's final conceptualization of Christ and the "regenerated" Albion as husbandmen, the mythos changes. As the apocalypse in Night Nine changes from the traditional one of Blake's earlier poetry so, ultimately, does Blake's myth. The apocalypse itself becomes something different from the transcendence of evil and chaos.

THREE

The Reassumption of Ancient Bliss

MIRCEA ELIADE says that all
the countless eschatological myths throughout the world cele-
brate the "repetition of the mythical moment of the passage
from chaos to cosmos": the end of the world followed by a re-
generation of life.[1] The believer in such a myth could experi-
ence this future regeneration *in the present* through ritual. This
ritual "reproduce[s] a primordial act . . . repeat[s] a mythical
example"[2] and reestablishes "sacred" time for the celebrant,
that time when the rhythms of the cosmos show the sacred
force behind that cosmos.[3] The ritual abolishes "profane" time
(that is, non-mythical time) for the worshipper, making him
"contemporary with the mythical moment of the beginning of
the world" so that he feels "the need of returning to that mo-
ment as often as possible in order to regenerate himself."[4]

Eliade's study of how rituals of regeneration "project [man]
into mythical time"[5] illuminates Blake's eschatological myth
in Night Nine, for as Urizen begins his husbandry on page
124, he and the other Zoas also begin performing an agricul-
tural ritual celebrating the creation of the cosmos out of chaos,
such as Eliade describes. Those archaic agricultural rituals of
which Eliade writes assumed the *necessity* of chaos for this crea-
tion of the cosmos, a point grasped with increasing clarity in
The Four Zoas. We can see this interplay between the polarities
of chaos and cosmos in Night Nine, as Antichrist *and* Christ
work to advance the apocalyptic "Regeneration" to come.
Night Nine opens with Christ standing invisibly next to Los

---

[1] Eliade, *The Myth of the Eternal Return*, p. 54.　　　[2] *Ibid.*, p. 4.

[3] Eliade, *Patterns in Comparative Religion*, p. 388.

[4] Eliade, *The Myth of the Eternal Return*, pp. 76-77.

[5] *Ibid.*, p. 58.

and Enitharmon as they build Jerusalem. We have, then, an archetype of the Self—and thus the possibility of psychic unity—intimated from the beginning of this Night. Although Los and Enitharmon heard the voice of Enion in 8.110.29, they evidently did not understand her message for, weeping, they believe Christ to be dead in the sepulchre. Los is motivated by his grief to start the apocalypse, so in a way Christ is responsible for its beginning, not Los.

Significantly, the image that Blake uses to describe this beginning of the end is the Yggdrasil, the World Tree of Norse mythology, which unites opposites with its roots in hell and its branches in the heavens. So Los:

> . . . his vegetable hands
> Outstretchd his right hand branching out in fibrous
>   Strength
> Siezd the Sun. His left hand like dark roots coverd the Moon
> And tore them down cracking the heavens across from
>   immense to immense.
>
> (9.117.6-9)

Los unifies the cosmic opposites of Sun and Moon, finally connecting them like the Yggdrasil with his "fibrous" hands.

Lines 9.119.1-23 give us the vigorous Antichrist seen earlier in Night Eight. In both passages the Antichrist destroys the wicked and aids the divine, certainly a change from the usual division of powers in the traditional apocalypse. As "loud the Serpent Orc ragd thro his twenty Seven Folds" blood pours from the sky in a scene reminiscent of the last plate of *Europe: A Prophecy*. Blood issuing from the sky as a divine judgment upon the wicked can be found in other accounts of the apocalypse, notably in *Revelation* 8:7-8 and 16:1-6. But in Blake's account this blood comes not from the divine sky but from Orc, who has become Urizen's agent, for it gushes in "torrents black" as a "black deluge," and the blood of snakes is traditionally considered black. Diverging further from tradition, this blood "cut[s] off . . . Tyranny . . . from the face of Earth" (9.119.14); so that Urizen eventually functions as an angel of the Lord. Furthermore, "around the Dragon form of Urizen" the "flames rolling intense thro the wide Universe Began to Enter the Holy City," and these "flames of mental fire" also work God's purpose as "the trembling millions" stand "bathing their Limbs in the bright visions of Eternity" (9.119.15-23).

Pages 120-123 prepare for Urizen's harrowing of the universe and the "Human Seed," and Blake's vision on page 123 of "the Son of Man" descending on a throne

> Of precious stones. surrounded by twenty four venerable
>   patriarchs
> And these again surrounded by four Wonders of the
>   Almighty.

$$(9.123.35-36)$$

is very similar to John's vision of God on his throne "of jasper . . . like unto an emerald," surrounded by "four and twenty elders" and "four beasts full of eyes before and behind" (*Rev.* 4:3-6): the four "Zoas" of Ezekiel's similar vision at Chebar. But Blake's own Zoas are more than simply angels of the Lord who empty God's "vials of wrath" upon mankind. Their actions rather seem to follow more from their desire to "Enter the Consummation" with Christ than because they are apocalyptic agents. They exist in "profane" time (as witness the allusions to contemporary events) and wish to experience "sacred" time:

> . . . in vain they strove to Enter the Consummation
> Together for the Redeemd Man could not enter the
>   Consummation
> Then siezd the Sons of Urizen the Plow . . .

$$(9.124.4-6)$$

Increasingly in *The Four Zoas* Blake has come to accept chaos as a polarity of the cosmos. Recalling Eliade's analysis of eschatological myths as celebrating the "passage from chaos to cosmos," we may see how pages 124-137 celebrate that passage, treating chaos as a necessary antinomy. The Zoas learn in

the course of these pages what Christ had tried to teach Los and
Enitharmon in the opening lines of the Night:

> Los & Enitharmon builded Jerusalem weeping
> Over the Sepulchre & over the Crucified body
> Which to their Phantom Eyes appear'd still in the Sepulcher
> But Jesus stood beside them in the Spirit Separating
> Their Spirit from their body. [They were] terrified at Non
>   Existence
> For such they deemd the death of the body.
>
> (9.117.1-6)

Running through these pages is a contrast between the per-
ception of the "Human Seed" and that of the Zoas. Until they
have become the "Bread of the Ages" and the "Human Wine,"
the humans have no comprehension of what is happening, and
simply exist in a state that Eliade would call "historical anxi-
ety," "howling" and "wailing." But the Zoas' actions have a
ceremonial quality suggesting that they understand the
"mythic" dimension of what they are doing and that they are
consciously performing steps in a ritual. Eliade shows how an-
cient agricultural religions tried through rituals to *contain*
chaos, seeing it as the background that makes possible "the
seasonal regeneration of the forces of the sacred. . . . The ritual
makes creation over again."[6] So begins on page 124 an agricul-
tural ritual of regeneration for the Zoas (and ultimately for
Albion) that will produce wine and bread, elements of the
Christian communion ritual, which also celebrates "sacred"
time while in "profane" time.

Urizen's plowing seems like the archaic ceremonial "driving
out of 'the old year' and . . . ills"[7] as he

> . . . drave the Plow of ages over Cities . . .
> Over the graves & caverns of the dead Over the Planets
> And over the void Spaces . . .   (9.124.26-29)

---

[6] Eliade, *Patterns in Comparative Religion*, pp. 345-46.
[7] *Ibid.*, p. 331.

with the "caverns of the dead" and "void spaces" thus becoming the fertile fields from which the grain will grow.

His sowing of the "Human Seed" may seem like mere cruel destruction, with "the myriads" of "immortal souls" cast by him into "the wide Universal field" where "in silent fear they look out from their graves" (9.125.21). However, human sacrifice is an extremely widespread custom associated with the sowing of the seed, a sympathetic magic in which life passes from man into the soil. This may sound like Blake's descriptions of the brutal bounty demanded by the "Goddess Nature" but it is not, for in its ritual context it implies ultimate rebirth for the sacrificed participant.

As Urizen and the sowers "repose till all the harvest is ripe," they are "entertained" by two "visions" reminding them of the rebirth from chaos which this unfolding agricultural rite celebrates. Ahania, who has dwelt in "death clothes" in "her darksom cave" as the "Human Seed" dwells in the "black mould" where Urizen has sown them, rises from the dead "like the harvest Moon." Her rebirth is followed by that of Luvah and Vala as they are finally reunited in a prelapsarian Eden. The episode becomes a momentary restoration of "the beginnings of time," showing what Eliade calls "the nostalgia for Paradise."[8] One might call it the Eliadean "archetype" of rebirth that the sowers' agricultural ritual is attempting to recreate.[9]

Vala's speech on pages 127-128 tells us at once that we are moving backward through time, for it is childlike in the extreme, and might be spoken by any of the narrators in *Songs of Innocence*. Since Vala was the "Demoness of Smoke" (9.126.4) before she was sent down by the sowers into this Edenic garden, the artifice of this diction becomes doubly apparent. Indeed, the movement of the episode in general is backward to

[8] *Ibid.*, p. 383.

[9] Eliade uses the word "archetype" to mean "an exemplary model" or "paradigm," and specifically denies that he intends to refer to the Jungian archetype on pp. viii-ix of the preface to the Torchbook edition (Harper and Row).

the beginnings of childhood, and as it proceeds its characters become increasingly younger rather than older. We first hear the adult Tharmas (who himself in the poem was the first Zoa to separate from his Emanation and, being associated with their falls, is also associated with the beginnings of time) lamenting his separation from Enion, as he has all through the poem. Here, however, he soon grows younger as he and Enion are magically reborn as Vala's children. The "little Boy" and "bright girl" revert even further toward their beginnings as Enion comes to seem "like the ruddy morn when infant spring appears," and follows Tharmas "in infant doubts" as the two play "in Eternal Childhood . . . In infant sorrow & joy alternate" (9.131.10-17).

The feast on page 133 after Urizen rises from his "repose" to use his "brazen sickle" and "scythe of iron" upon the "human harvest" is similar to end-of-the-harvest feasts whose symbolic function was to focus the vital energy released in the harvest upon humanity.[10] Thus the "Eternals" who are at the "golden feast" speak of the human community of "Brotherhood & Universal Love," predicting that man, though "cast . . . like a Seed into the Earth," will eventually be reborn as "Man liveth not by Self alone but in his brothers face Each shall behold the Eternal Father & love & joy abound" (9.133.25-26).

The orgy on pages 135-137, which follows this vision of spiritual rebirth, may seem to contrast grotesquely with the solemnity of the creation of the "wine of the Ages" and the "bread of the Ages," not to mention the final glorious "Regeneration" of Zoas and Albion. In Blake's orgy, Luvah with his sons and daughters drunkenly trample the "Human vintage" in the "terrible winepresses of Luvah" and presumably all incestuously copulate "laughing & shouting drunk with odors" as they "lay them on skins of tygers or the spotted Leopard or wild Ass" (9.136.17-19). Tharmas and Urthona likewise "r[i]se from the Golden feast satiated with Mirth & Joy." Luvah and Vala (thoroughly drunk by now) fall asleep on the

---

[10] Eliade, *Patterns in Comparative Religion*, pp. 349-50.

floor and "Luvah [is] put for dung on the ground by the Sons of Tharmas & Urthona" (9.137.24). Yet the orgy was another end-of-the-harvest ritual occurring all over the world. Eliade makes an ingenious parallel between the decomposing seed which loses its original form in the chaos of the earth to be reborn as new vegetation, and the orgiastic celebrant who likewise abolishes all individuality, constraint, and law to be similarly reborn.[11] In other words, the orgy was another ritual containment of chaos and celebrated the rebirth of the cosmos. I certainly do not mean to suggest that Blake deliberately sought to reproduce these archaic agricultural rituals in Night Nine; indeed, I strongly believe that the connection was unconscious, and can be seen only by considering these pages in the context of the previous Nights and their patterns of archetypes. The general concept of time underlying these archaic agricultural religions is one Blake came to espouse, whether consciously or not. For during the long period of composition of *The Four Zoas*, his concept of time and history changed from the linear Judaic concept of his earlier poetry, which saw human history progressing toward an end in which the faithful remnant will be reunited with God. Rather, Blake's conception of time now regards generation, death, and regeneration as aspects of a universal process that keeps repeating itself.

Eliade calls this latter view of time "cyclical," a word that can cause misunderstanding if applied to Blake's mythos without caution. On the face of it, "cyclical" time may sound like Blake's "same dull round" of natural religion (*There Is No Natural Religion*, Conclusion), the "cycle of nature" from which Blake says man is to be delivered. One hazard of writing about Blake is that frequently he uses key terms in a special sense, so that the critic must redefine those words when using them for his own, non-Blakean purposes. Eliade says that the archaic view of time is one in which death and decay are accepted as part of the process of the "eternal return." "The death of the individual and the *periodic* death of humanity are necessary . . .

[11] *Ibid.*, pp. 356-59.

for their regeneration. . . . What predominates . . : is the cy-
clical recurrence of what has been before, in a word, eternal re-
turn. . . . The cyclical structure of time . . . is regenerated at
each new 'birth.' "[12] The connotations of "cycle" are dynamic
for Eliade; they are static for Blake.

Blake's sense of the word may be seen in "The Mental
Traveller" (written during the middle period of *The Four Zoas'*
composition). This nightmarish poem does not show the
movement between polarities of existence that is implicit in
Eliade's description of archaic time, but rather a fixed round in
the "fallen" world in which the "Contraries" are never even
experienced. Death is not really accepted by either man or
woman, for as each grows old each battens on the youth of the
other. Regeneration is certainly not possible for anyone in the
poem, for all are imaginatively bound to the world of Genera-
tion both in Blake's and Eliade's sense of that word. Eliade
would probably say that the man and woman are caught in
"historical" time that has no conception of the "eternal" di-
mension of existence.

Eliade's sense of "cycle" may be seen in the final lines of
Jerusalem (to anticipate a fuller discussion of the apocalypse of
this poem). Certainly Blake did not intend in this grand con-
cluding portrayal of man's "awaking to Eternal Life" (*J*1.4.2)
to show the supremacy of the "cycle of nature," yet it illus-
trates the Eliadean process of the "eternal return" as

> All Human Forms identified even Tree Metal Earth &
> Stone. all
> Human Forms identified, living, going forth & returning
> wearied
> Into the Planetary lives of Years Months Days & Hours
> reposing
> And then Awaking into his Bosom in the Life of
> Immortality.
>
> (*J*4.99.1-4)

[12] Eliade, *The Myth of the Eternal Return*, pp. 88-89.

This concept of the "eternal return" supposes the necessity of mutability for rebirth, an assumption that underlies the conclusion of *The Four Zoas.*

Significant of this assumption is the fact that elements previously associated with the Antichrist *become part of the ritual,* from the very beginning on page 124, as Urizen begins his plowing. It seems likely that this event was intended to contrast with Urizen's construction of the Mundane Shell in the beginning of Night Two, for Blake's description of both activities is very similar. We may see why Urizen's present attempt is successful, where that in Night Two was not, if we consider the manner in which it is done. For one thing, he uses pre-industrial instruments rather than the "compasses, the quadrant & the rule & the balance" of Night Two. But there are other, different, elements in Urizen's plowing in Night Nine. He begins it directly after trying to "Enter the Consummation" with a Christ who has become very real in the poem, and after Urizen has experienced possession by the other aspect of that archetype. The harness that Urizen uses in the plowing also combines these antinomies, for it is "ornamented With beautiful art the study of angels the workmanship of Demons When Heaven & Hell in Emulation strove in sports of Glory" (9.124.11-13). Those animals in the "desarts & rocks" who had been animated by Urizen-as-Antichrist in Night Eight now work with Urizen in Night Nine to begin the plowing as "the horses neigh . . . the wild bulls from the sultry waste The tygers from the forests & the lions from the sandy desarts . . . give . . . to Urthonas Sons . . . the spade the mattock & the ax" (9.124.15-21).

The pastoral episode following this plowing shows a paradise in which "ancient innocence" is restored. In a very real way, its poetic diction captures the "nostalgia for paradise" of which Eliade writes, for its viewpoint is that of a child who sees paradise in all of its surroundings. Vala expresses a fear of mortality and the yearning for rebirth, but without much more depth of comprehension than any of Blake's earlier Innocents. The language of this episode is undeniably beautiful, a kind of restoration within the poem of the Songs from Blake's own "ancient innocence." Yet this profusion of melody should not keep us from seeing that the episode is counterpoised emotionally against those recent and powerful chants of Ahania and Enion at the end of Night Eight, which describe the same situation as that of the pastoral episode. It takes an effort to realize that when Vala says to Luvah:

> O thou fair one . . . thou art as the grass
> Thou risest in the dew of morning & at night art folded
>   up
>
> (9.127.14-15)

her meaning is essentially the same as Ahania's when the latter cries:

> Will you seek pleasure from the festering wound or marry
>   for a Wife
> The ancient Leprosy that the King & Priest may still feast
>   on your decay
>
> (8.108.13-14)

Ahania's cry in Night Eight of "the dark body of corruptible death" and Enion's answering chant of "Man {as} . . . in pain he sighs in pain he labours in his universe" resonate beneath this pastoral scene of Night Nine. For this scene in Night Nine is preoccupied with the same questions of mutability and death as the rest of *The Four Zoas*. Later, when Vala goes to bathe in the river, she hears the "mournful voice" of Tharmas with the burden of dissociation and grief that his laments have had all through the rest of the poem:

> O Enion my weary head is in the bed of death
> For weeds of death have wrapd around my limbs in the
>   hoary deeps . . .
> When will the time of Clouds be past & the dismal night of
>   Tharmas
>
> (9.129.20-23)

Even in this paradise, this "re-creation of the Cosmos," mutability and chaos exist as elements present from the beginning.

There is the balancing promise of rebirth held out to Vala and Tharmas, as it was to Enion in Night Eight. Someone—Luvah, clearly, but it could as well be Urizen or Christ—promises Vala that:

> Yon Sun shall wax old & decay but thou shalt ever flourish
> The fruit shall ripen & fall down & the flowers consume
>   away
> But thou shalt still survive arise O dry thy dewy tears.
> (9.127.25-27)

Tharmas and Enion are finally reunited as children. Yet even in this paradise, Enion still flees from him initially. And one may wonder how Vala will feel when those creatures and flowers with which she identifies so closely in her pastoral wanderings ("my flocks you are my brethren," "you birds . . . you are my sisters") *do* "wax old & decay."

Yet although this is all so, this episode is different from any other presentation of chaos in the poem, and indeed "entertain[s] . . . the sleepers upon the Couches of Beulah." One should recall Urizen's speech as he places Luvah and Vala in this "Garden" in 9.126.9-17: if the fallen Zoas would "resume the image of the human" they must "renew their brightness" and start again as children. And so no one in "Valas Garden" has any more knowledge of change or death than did the Zoas at the beginning of Night One. The great difference here—the difference making rebirth possible—is that no one struggles any longer against the experience of chaos. The pervading tone of the episode is *pliancy*, rather than the resisting terror that the Zoas and Emanations felt upon first encountering this polarity. Vala's reaction to "Eternal Death" is:

> Alas am I but as a flower then will I sit me down
> Then will I weep then Ill complain & sigh for immortality
> And chide my maker thee O sun that raisedst me to fall.
> (9.127.16-18)

When Tharmas mourns in his river, "O Enion my weary head is in the bed of death," he no longer raves of love turning to hatred, as in 3.45.11, or of suicide, as in 6.69.8-22, but rather says, "Arise O Enion arise for Lo I have calmd my seas" (9.129.27). It is the inward psychological experience of the characters here rather than their touchingly innocent outward actions that "entertains," their openness to experience of either polarity: either "that sweet & comforting voice" or "that voice of sorrow" (9.127.28-29).

This pastoral episode functions as a mandala within the poem, both for the Zoas and for the reader as well. It is extended in length and literally occupies a central position in pages 124-137. It has proved peculiarly haunting for readers of the poem, with almost all critics commenting on its beauty and calling it a vision of Beulah. Created in the midst of the "terrible confusion of the wracking universe," this "Garden" incorporates just those dark elements that have caused such anguish outside and balances them with the bright promise of rebirth and reintegration in Christ. The chants of Ahania and Enion, considered together, might seem to do the same. Those pages (8.108 and 8.109) are not a mandala, however, because a sense of restless sorrow remains in the language and suggests that order and harmony are not yet truly created.

However, the diction and texture of the language on pages 127-131 of Night Nine *do* create this feeling of order, as do the characters' tranquil attitudes of mind. It seems clear that Blake intended to create this sense of order in the reader as well as in the "sleepers rest[ing] from their harvest work," for there is an accumulation of details that seem to have as their main purpose the creation of a mood so that (as literally as is possible with a mental act) "the Spectator . . . could Enter into Noahs Rainbow . . . and make . . . a Companion of . . . these Images of wonder."[13] There is the long opening monologue by Vala which allows the reader to merge with her perception of the scene about her, creating an immediate identity with that perception. The very language used by Blake throughout the

[13] *P & P*, p. 550.

episode is monosyllabic and direct, further decreasing any sense of distance between reader and Vala.

This feeling of stability produced by the episode renews the characters within the poem also, for Urizen rises on page 131 after seeing it and cries, "Times are Ended"—words ushering in the harvesting and vintage of the "Human Seed." This harvest causes the "Seed" to experience the same despair as the Zoas had experienced in Night Eight, when it seemed that the Antichrist controlled all, and Enion chants her fuller vision here as there. Voicing that despair (speaking in her own voice and certainly not that of the "girl" in "Valas Garden"), she says:

> O Dreams of Death the human form dissolving companied
> By beasts & worms & creeping things & darkness & despair
> $$\text{(9.132.18-19)}$$

in an echo of the "Visions of Ahania" in Night Eight. She answers the despair of the "Human Harvest" as she had answered Ahania earlier, declaring the resurrection of just those "scaly monsters," "worms" and "devouring serpents" that had filled Ahania's visions. This passage in Night Nine is the first to describe the beginning of the prophesied "new Heaven and new earth," and significantly the elements of nature that "cr[y] To one another What are we & whence is our joy & delight" are those chthonic creatures associated in Night Eight with the Antichrist:

> . . . the jointed worm
> . . . the scaly newt [that] creeps
> From the stone & the armed fly [that] springs from the
>   rocky crevice
> The spider. The bat [that] burst from the hardend slime.
> $$\text{(9.132.26-31)}$$

They "cry out in joys of existence," much as did those other animals associated with unconscious energy that the Antichrist reanimated in Night Eight: the lion, the bear, the wild stag, and the horse.

When we study these pages on which the "Human Grape" is harvested, we can begin to understand how far beyond the traditional Judeo-Christian apocalypse Blake has moved, how far beyond his own earlier conception of it he has moved. This harvest grows increasingly violent and formless, culminating in the "treading of the Human Grape," which remarkably resembles the song of the Females of Amalek in Night Eight. This part of the harvesting has proved troublesome for some critics because (no matter how one interprets it) one cannot ignore the fact that Blake is presenting a clinical case of sadism as a necessary, even desirable, part of "Regeneration." It was generally understood by apocalyptists that the distress of the faithful remnant will be severe, but not that the performing angels of the Lord would consider such suffering as "the sports of love & . . . the sweet delights of amorous play" (9.137.2). Eliade has his own interpretation of the orgy as a ritual containment of chaos, useful as an explanation, yet still in its cerebral abstraction suggesting that that learned scholar's own discipline of the history of religions does not ask for the fieldwork required in the related discipline of anthropology. Luvah's harvesting of the grapes proves to be consistent with Blake's own changing myth, however, complementing Urizen's harvesting of the grain and continuing the psychological odyssey begun in "Valas Garden." The "Human Forms" began life in that garden as children who were embryonically one with their pastoral surroundings; here, they proceed further toward maturity as they descend into the unconscious and experience the horrors, libidinous appetites, and life-giving energies which exist there.

The harvesting of the grapes begins with a sensuous passage that seems as limpid as the pastoral scene in "Valas Garden" with the "flocks [with] wooly backs" and "delicious . . . grapes flourishing in the Sun." Yet the animals here have a fury and energy that is lacking in that other setting, barely controlled in the beginning of the harvest as the "flocks & herds trample the Corn" and the "cattle browse upon The ripe Clusters." The bull and lion that started Urizen's plowing begin Luvah's harvest here, but are not (Blake promises) creatures that should be feared ultimately, for the bull "lick[s] the little girls white neck" and "the lion of terror . . . eat[s] from the curld boys white lap . . . and in the evening sleep[s] before the Door" (9.135.16-20).

As the "Human Grapes" descend into the unconscious, Luvah changes his mien accordingly. There has been a running association between Luvah and Christ throughout *The Four Zoas*, with Christ frequently appearing in "Luvahs robes of blood." The martyrdom of the Zoa shut up in the furnaces suggests that other martyrdom, and the Zoa's name implies the Son of Love also. Recently in "Valas Garden" Luvah appeared as "the fair one" for whom Vala searches, and throughout the episode her quest echoes that of the bride in *The Song of Songs* for the bridegroom, who is traditionally interpreted as symbolizing Christ. At this later point in the Night, however, Luvah seems more like Dionysus than Christ as "his crown of thorns [falls] from his head" and he makes his drunken way to the winepress with all of its hellish tortures waiting for the "Human Grapes" in his control. It takes no particular acuity to see this parallel between Luvah and Dionysus. However, it should be noted that although Dionysus is usually associated with the irrational and libidinous powers of the unconscious, he is also connected with Christ. Jung considers Christ himself (mythically speaking) to have gained knowledge of the unconscious when he harrowed Hell prior to his resurrection. Many historians of religion consider the worship of Dionysus to have been gradually modified through syncretism as the cult spread outwards from Greece, to become the quieter and more mystical cult of Orphism, and that this widely disseminated religion in turn had affinities with Christianity. One may say that, archetypally, Dionysus, Orpheus, and Christ all represent the same figure of the god-man who is slain, descends to the underworld, and then is resurrected, as his followers will be if they partake of his mysteries.

Luvah and his sons bring the wagons of gathered grapes to the winepresses, and the scene grows closer in spirit to that final plate of *Europe: A Prophecy*, where the "Lions lash[ed] their wrathful tails! the Tigers . . . suck[ed] the ruddy tide," and the "golden chariots rag[ed] with red wheels dropping with blood." Blake's imagination took him no further in *Europe: A Prophecy*; here, these elements of wrath and bloodthirsty violence are absorbed into the greater process unfolding as:

> . . . ramping tygers play
> In the jingling traces furious lions sound the song of joy
> To the golden wheels circling . . . all
> The Villages of Luvah . . .
> Reply to violins & tabors to the pipe flute lyre & cymbal
>
> (9.135.29-33)

These wheels lead to the dropping of blood, too, as we see in the lines immediately following, in which the "Clusters of human families" fall from the wagons into the winepress, and "the blood of life flowd plentiful" as those "human families" enter "the caverns of the Grave."

"Assume the dark Satanic body in the Virgins womb O Lamb divine," chanted the sons of Eden in Night Eight as they "beh[e]ld the Wonders of the Grave," and in response the Females of Amalek sang their terrible song. In Night Nine, the "Human Odors" sing briefly in *their* "Caverns of the Grave," and then experience what the victims of the Females of Amalek experienced; and here as in Night Eight, what seems to be a manifestation of the Antichrist is incorporated into the process of Regeneration rather than being cast out. The experience of the "Grapes" in the winepress is a miniature of the Zoas' falls during the previous Nights, and they too face the "dreadful Non Existence" that Zoas and Emanations have known. But the "Grapes" are wiser than the Zoas were, for the "Grapes" call for the waiting torments rather than trying to avoid them. They cry, "Let us consume in fires In waters stifling or in air corroding or in earth shut up" (9.136.13-14), thus seeking the elements into which each of the Zoas has fallen in the first eight Nights.

Like bacchants and bacchantes, the sons and daughters of

Luvah "tread the Grapes," "drowned in the wine," and lie
down on skins of animals associated with Dionysus or his ret-
inue.[14] Characteristic of this scene is lack of any restraint on
their instincts as energy flows in all directions. Sadism too,
with its shifting blend of pleasure and pain, is part of this play
of instincts, which may explain that "cruel joy of Luvah's
daughters" and those "deadly sports of Luvahs sons." This
libidinous aspect of the unconscious is not far from what Orc
in his Caves knew (and note that the sons and daughters cele-
brate near "cool Grots") as the flames

> Dance[d] on the rivers & the rocks howling & drunk with
>   fury
> The plow of ages & the golden harrow wade[d] thro fields
> Of goary blood.
>
> (7.77.13-15)

The "Human Grapes" experience the other, more negative
side of the unconscious in the winepress. Blake describes their
experience as

> They howl & writhe in shoals of torment in fierce Flames
>   consuming
> In chains of iron & in dungeons circled with ceaseless fires
> In pits & dens & shades of death.
>
> (9.136.22-24)

and hints that their falls mirror the Zoas' previous descents
into the unconscious: Tharmas' "shoals of torment" in the sea,
Luvah's "fierce flames consuming" in his furnaces, Los's
"chains of iron" that bound him through jealousy to Orc, and
Urizen's "pits & dens & shades of death" that he explored as he
fell downward toward Ulro.

But we are left with a final positive picture of the uncon-
scious, as Blake gives us those renewed creatures that dance
around the winepress. As earth's lowly creatures were resur-

---

[14] Dionysus in one of his many travels crossed the Tigris on a tiger given
to him by Zeus; Bacchus was frequently accompanied by leopards; and
Silenus was generally shown riding an ass.

rected while Urizen was harvesting the grain, so creatures that
are even closer to the underground are regenerated while Luvah
harvests the grapes. The earthworm, centipede, ground spider,
mole, earwig, maggot, slug, grasshopper, nettle, and thistle
appear "naked in all their beauty dancing round the Wine
Presses." Blake reveals the beauty of these chthonic beings in
his description of the "Mole clothed in Velvet," "the tender
maggot emblem of Immortality," the grasshopper with "slen-
der bones," and the nettle with its "soft down."

In Night Eight, Urizen displayed all of the power and bril-
liance of the archetype of the Antichrist, and then sank in
prominence as the unconscious threatened all with its "indefi-
nite lust." There was an anticlimactic descent from the vigor-
ous energy with which Urizen "flame[d] with wrath &
majesty" and "lash[ed] the Abyss," as his appearance turned
the other Zoas to stone pillars that rolled round and round—a
far distance from his animation of the lion and bear who
"cr[ied] out in terrible existence." In Night Nine, the uncon-
scious again threatens dominance as the sons and daughters of
Luvah begin to squabble among themselves, "quite exhausted
with the Labour & quite filld with new wine." Luvah declines
as Urizen did, changing from Dionysus to Silenus as he sleeps
drunkenly on the floor.

The wine is made. It remains for the bread to be created.
Los is "regenerated" as Urthona and, together with Tharmas,
grinds and bakes the bread in a process duplicating the vintage
of the wine. This is a comparatively brief passage in which the
"Human Grain" suffers as did the "Human Grapes," once
more duplicating the falls of the Zoas as the mills of Urthona
are turned by "Thunders Earthquakes Fires Water floods." Yet
these first fifteen lines of page 138 have an added significance
in *The Four Zoas* if one remembers pages 87-90 in Night
Seven, where Los as "binder of the sheaves" created his
"mighty circle." There as here, order was created out of chaos
while *using* that chaos as a source of energy. There is the
suggestion here that Urthona will be able to do this as he first
rises "in all his regenerate power" prior to the grinding of the
grain, and:

The Sea that rolld & foamd with darkness & the shadows
    of death
Vomited out & gave up all the floods . . .
Singing & shouting to the Man they bow their hoary
    heads
And murmuring in their channels flow & circle
    round his feet

                                        (9.137.35-38)

So Urthona's circular mills grind the grain, using as energy the
unabated violence of the "whirlwinds" and the "stormy seas
. . . Eddying fierce [and] rejoic[ing] in the fierce agitation of
the wheels Of Dark Urthona" (9.138.5-7).

The sufferings of the "Human Grain" in Urthona's mills
parallel those of the "Human Grapes" in Luvah's winepresses.
"The Plates the Screws and Racks & Saws & cords" that the
"Grapes" knew in the winepresses seemed straight from the
song of the Females of Amalek, who appeared as the Antichrist
materialized. Similarly, the torments suffered from the
"Grain" recall those that Urizen announced to Orc as the latter
changed into his serpentine guise of the Antichrist in Night
Seven:

    . . . when a man looks pale
    With labour & abstinence say he looks healthy & happy
    And when his children sicken let them die there are enough
    Born even too many & our Earth will be overrun
    Without these arts

                                        (7.80.10-14)

That terrible indictment of Blake's contemporary utilitarian-
ism, and more specifically Malthusianism, is echoed in Night
Nine as the "Grain" endures the mental equivalent of the
"Grapes" agony:

    . . . Men are bound to sullen contemplations in the night
        . . .
    . . . in their inmost brain
    Feeling the crushing Wheels they rise they write the bitter
        words

Of Stern Philosophy & knead the bread of knowledge with
   tears & groans

(9.138.12-15)

The bread is thus made, and lies waiting "in golden & in
silver baskets." Both elements of the ritual now exist. Urthona
is about to resume his dominion over the "bright Universe
Empery" that he had "attended day & night" in the opening
lines of the poem, finally—one hundred and thirty-eight pages
later—"ris[ing] . . . in all his ancient strength to form the
golden armour of science" (9.139.7-8). But intervening are
twenty lines that make *possible* this resumption of "ancient
strength," giving as they do Blake's final portrayal of Albion's
"regenerated" imaginative perception. It is not a vision that
has been present before in Blake's myth.

What Albion sees is the "eternal return," the cycle of gener-
ation, death, and regeneration that the Zoas have just cele-
brated in their agricultural rituals. As Eliade predicts of the
celebrant who experiences "sacred" time, Albion sees the
power behind the cosmos that manifests itself in the rhythms
of that cosmos.[15] He sees "the Stars Of fire rise up nightly
from the Ocean & one Sun Each morning like a New born Man
issues with songs & Joy (9.138.27-28), that night voyage sig-
nifying the psyche's passage through death to new life, through
the unconscious to consciousness. Man participates in these
natural rhythms as he "walks upon the Eternal Mountains rais-
ing his heavenly voice Conversing with the Animal forms of
wisdom night & day" (9.138.30-31).

What Albion beholds is the play of polarities. His vision
here is of a *perpetual process* rather than the final event of tradi-
tional eschatology, for as the Zoas' previous rituals have
created Albion's "mythic time," so these rituals are here con-
tinually recurrent. They *maintain* the apocalypse:

. . . Tharmas brought his flocks upon the hills & in
   the Vales

---

[15] Eliade, *Patterns in Comparative Religion*, p. 388.

Around the Eternal Mans bright tent the little Children
   play
Among the wooly flocks The hammer of Urthona sounds.
                              (9.138.33-35)

This cyclical process is continued in the concluding page as
Albion's vision is translated into reality and "the Sun arises
. . . the fresh airs play . . . the fresh Earth beams forth," and
Urthona finally rises (no longer divided into Los and Enithar-
mon). He is ready

For intellectual War The war of swords departed now
The dark Religions are departed & sweet Science reigns.
                              (9.139.9-10)

So ends *The Four Zoas*. Albion and his Zoas have at last been
"resurrect[ed] to Unity"—and that "Unity" proves to be
"War," the war of "Contraries" about which Blake wrote so
long ago in *The Marriage of Heaven and Hell*.

FOUR

Going Forth to the Vintage
of Nations

*M*ilton requires a psychological analysis more than any other of Blake's poems, for if *The Four Zoas* takes place in Albion's "circling Nerves" (*FZ* 1.11.15), *Milton* is quite intentionally enacted in Blake's own "Human Brain." *The Four Zoas* had explored the general nature of the unconscious, seeking to discover what it *is*. One of the many remarkable aspects of that poem was its unerring accuracy in giving us the very workings of the unconscious, both in dramatic actions and in symbols. *Milton* advances to examine the unconscious as it acts within Blake himself, the individual man who was a poet staying at a cottage in Felpham under the patronage of a generous dullard.[1] Bloom calls the poem "genuinely purgatorial";[2] one can go further and say that it is Blake's own harrowing of hell. Using Jungian psychology to study this poem does not reduce its aesthetic value; on the contrary, it helps us to see how artistic form works to incorporate the unconscious into the work of art. Most clearly in *this* poem archetypes act as they do in the psychology of the individual, and ultimately the result is *Jerusalem*.

I am not attempting in this reading of *Milton* to use Blake's art to psychoanalyze the man: "Aha! Here one can clearly see symptoms of neurosis or even psychosis, for *I* can understand things in the work of art of which the mere artist was not at all aware." (Jung himself comments after discussing the dangers for patients of psychic inflation during analysis, "Psychoanaly-

---

[1] See Morchard Bishop's book, *Blake's Hayley: The Life, Works, and Friendships of William Hayley,* for a necessary corrective to the usual portrait of Hayley as a sinister philistine conspiring to smother Blake.

[2] *P & P*, p. 823.

sis itself has this same bland unconsciousness of its limitations, as can clearly be seen from the way it meddles with works of art."[3]) But Blake was using art to understand what was happening to him psychologically; the only difference was that instead of using abstract analytic theories he used equally abstract allegory. *Milton* is not the cast-off garment of the reborn who has moved forward into the future, but rather an immediate celebration of the very action of rebirth *as it is happening in the creation of the poem.*

The poem as a whole is an exploration of Blake's own unconscious, and is twofold in structure: in the Bard's Song, Blake examines his own personal unconscious; in the rest of the poem, he searches out his own experience of the collective unconscious. Jung says that an individual reveals himself primarily in the pattern of archetypes to be seen in the dreams and fantasies. If we consider the archetypes that dominate *Milton*, we may see several things: how Blake manages to avoid the real danger of psychic inflation as he identifies with Milton; what the immediate and continuing function of the poem is for Blake as he writes it and as he reads it afterwards; and why Blake always puts such great stress on the political present in his poetry.

Milton seems to follow so closely the general process by which Jung says a person reaches individuation that it is best to examine what Jung has to say on the subject. The individual variations are endless, of course, but still there are quite definite steps to individuation. Gradually one familiarizes oneself with the unconscious, first the personal unconscious and then (with much more difficulty) the collective unconscious.

The first stage is recognizing the distinction between one's persona and one's more individual nature. The word "persona" has passed into general parlance, but it is well to define it as Jung defines it: "a mask that *feigns individuality*, making others and oneself believe that one is individual, whereas one is simply acting a role through which the collective psyche speaks,"[4]

[3] Jung, *Two Essays*, p. 141.
[4] *Ibid.*, p. 157.

"designed on the one hand to make a definite impression upon others, and, on the other, to conceal the true nature of the individual."[5] Jung states categorically that "the dissolution of the persona is . . . an indispensable condition for individuation . . . Only when the unconscious is assimilated [the unconscious that has been repressed by the persona] does the individuality emerge more clearly."[6]

Recognition of one's Shadow is more painful, but still not too difficult, since it is also closely connected with the personal unconscious. If the persona hides the signs of one's personal unconscious from others (which are not generally received by others as pleasant experiences), then the Shadow is the dark side that the persona is designed to conceal. These Shadow characteristics seem to have an *emotional* nature, a kind of autonomy, a possessive quality.[7] Jung calls the comprehension of the Shadow "a *moral* problem that challenges the whole ego-personality,"[8] and while Freud probably would not approve of this introduction of such an "unscientific" area as morality into psychoanalysis, Blake certainly would.

The Shadow is fairly accessible to consciousness; it is far more difficult to become aware of the presence of the archetype of the anima (or the animus, for the woman). It appears as a projection, which might seem to belong to the Shadow but does not, since it refers to the opposite sex; and it filters "the contents of the collective unconscious through to the conscious mind."[9] This archetype has been discussed in Chapter Two. I will add only that she is much further away from consciousness than the Shadow (and consequently harder to recognize as a projection rather than an objective reality).

Each stage evolves into the next, and the man's recognition of his anima gives rise, says Jung, to a triad: "the masculine subject [himself], the opposing feminine subject [the actual opposite sex], and the transcendent anima."[10] There is a missing fourth element of the personality, for wholeness (as Jung

[5] *Ibid*., p. 192.　　　　　　　[6] *Ibid*., p. 297.

[7] Jung, *Aion*, p. 8.　　　　　　[8] *Ibid*., p. 8. Emphasis added.

[9] *Ibid*., p. 20.　　　　　　　　[10] *Ibid*., p. 22.

sees it) is symbolically expressed by quaternity: that missing element, for men, is the archetype of the Wise Old Man, the supramasculine figure whose knowledge helps the man toward an understanding of the unified Self he may achieve. These four elements of the male personality together make up the archetype of the *marriage quaternio*, a "schema" of the self.[11]

Blake's three-year stay at Felpham has proved a favorite occasion for biographers and critics alike to show their man as the dazzling gem against the grey velveteen of Hayley and his friends, and there is no need to set forth that familiar sight here. Still, the extent to which Hayley was a deadly accurate parody of Blake himself is quite uncanny. This is probably one reason why the experience shook Blake as it did, even beyond those obvious practical circumstances which by themselves could explain a man driven close to paranoia.[12] There was a remarkable symmetry about the situation. Hayley's friends called Hayley a "true poet" with "the fire and invention of Dryden" whose "numbers [were] sweet and flowing."[13] He composed rapidly and profusely upon the most lofty of subjects, and moreover was proficient in watercolors and miniature painting. This man was patron and taskmaster of Blake, who in his few years at Lambeth had created both cosmogony and apocalypse in that staggering output of Books, Prophecies, and early version of *Vala*, and whose artistic stature was equally commanding. Hayley lacked Blake's genius and his saving tough grace of humor. But could it not have occurred to Blake in his worst moments during that long and isolated stay that he might not be so very different from Hayley, a mirror image in a fun house? In fact, in the eyes of the world (and probably Hayley himself) Blake must have seemed like the double of Hayley.

[11] *Ibid.*, p. 22.

[12] See Keynes, ed., *Letters of William Blake*, p. 63; Helms, "Blake at Felpham: A Study in the Psychology of Vision"; and Erdman, *Prophet*, p. 105.

[13] Hayley's friend Anna Seward in a letter: Wilson, *The Life of William Blake*, p. 145.

Not only can Hayley be seen as the suitable persona for Blake to emulate according to polite—and well-off—British society (for Hayley even managed to secure an annuity for his poetry from his publisher), but there were other ways in which the "collective psyche" was speaking through the situation. There are many hints that some of Blake's friends hoped that life at Felpham would modify Blake's craziness so as to bring him more into line with what was sensible. Flaxman (who had introduced Blake to Hayley) wrote to Hayley: "Indeed I hope that Blake's residence at Felpham will be a Mutual Comfort to you & him, & I see no reason why he should not make as good a livelihood there as at London, if he engraves & teaches drawing . . . making neat drawings of different kinds but if he places any dependence on painting large pictures, for which he is not qualified, either by habit or study, he will be miserably decieved."[14] Blake's old friend Thomas Butts commented in a letter to Blake: "this I predict, that you will be a better Man . . . [that] certain opinions imbibed from reading, nourish'd by indulgence, and rivetted by a confined Conversation, and which have been equally prejudicial to your Interest & Happiness, will now, I trust, disperse as a Day-break Vapour, and you will henceforth become a Member of [the] Community."[15]

The very presence of a persona indicates an ability to deceive oneself about oneself, a social skill that Blake had lacked from the beginning. Blake's honesty—his desire to set down what *he* was as well as what others seemed to be—was one of his most persistent traits. Consider, for example, the Lambeth Books and Prophecies. On the one hand, we can see in them the shifting cloudy outlines of a gigantic myth that would explain all of human existence past and present, as well as call through etching and trumpet-verse for the hastening of the imminent millennium. But on the other hand, we can see just as clearly the strong, almost grotesque satire upon the mythmaker who would fossilize the world, and the portrayal of

[14] *Ibid.*, p. 150.
[15] Keynes, ed., *Letters of William Blake*, p. 44.

the darker side of the millennium from the viewpoint of the innocent as well as the king. It seems likely that part of Blake's crisis at Felpham was a conflict between his real individual nature and a persona collectively approved by all of those socially and politically powerful people about him who were well-meaning (that was the worst of it) and pragmatically wise. Consider Blake's letter to Butts in early 1802 when the whole affair was nearly over:

"But if we fear to do the dictates of our Angels, & tremble at the Tasks set before us; if we refuse to do Spiritual Acts because of Natural Fears or Natural Desires! Who can describe the dismal torments of such a state!—I too well remember the Threats I heard!—If you, who are organised by Divine Providence for Spiritual communion, Refuse, & bury your Talent in the Earth, even tho' you should want Natural Bread, Sorrow & Desperation pursues you thro' life, & after death Shame & confusion of face to eternity. Everyone in Eternity will leave you."[16]

We should remember those "Natural Fears" staring Blake in the face, before too easily rejoicing that our hero of course did not succumb to collective mediocrity: fear of paupery and possible starvation (a literal enough fear in the late eighteenth century), fear of losing the only real patron of fortune that Blake ever found, fear of England's increasingly repressive political climate at that time (brought home nicely by the Scofield incident). Poor Catherine Blake. Blake's prophecy in fact came quite true, for during the rest of their lives back in London later the Blakes "want[ed] Natural Bread . . . & Desperation pursue[d them] thro' life, & after death Shame & confusion of face" surrounded Blake's reputation for over a century. He lacked only "Sorrow."

The Bard's Song in *Milton* has troubled a good many critics, some of whom see it as simply obscure.[17] It is obviously im-

---

[16] *Ibid.*, p. 56.

[17] In Curran and Wittreich, eds., *Blake's Sublime Allegory*, see W.J.T. Mitchell, "Blake's Radical Comedy: Dramatic Structure as Meaning in *Mil-*

portant in the scheme of the poem, since it "at length mov'd
Milton to [his] unexampled deed" (1.2.21) of descending from
Heaven to search for Ololon, and eventually merge with Blake
at poem's end. But it would be totally obscure for the reader if
he did not know the inner and outer particulars of Blake's life
at Felpham—and what is the point of going over all that any-
way, since Blake must have triumphed over the associated
agony and humiliation in order to keep on writing *Milton* at
all? The answer must be that Blake had not yet triumphed
while he was writing the Song, and that its presence in the
poem is somehow necessary for the poem to go on.

There is more to the Song than Blake's rendering in allegory
of that experience which proved so crucially self-defining for
him. It is not until plate 7 of the ten-plate Song that Blake
devotes all of his attention to the argument between Satan and
Palamabron, although there are a few brief passages referring
to it earlier. Bloom comments that the difficulties in *Milton* lie
mainly in the "problems of continuity and . . . sudden changes
of perspective,"[18] to be seen in these opening plates of Book
One.

The "Bard broke forth . . . terrific among the Sons of Albion
in chorus solemn & loud" (1.2.23-24), and how does this
"Prophetic Song" begin? With an account of the cosmogony to
be sure, but one which is almost wearyingly familiar to us by
this time, as Los again begins working with that "red round
Globe hot burning" (1.3.11). Again "it separate[s] into a Male
Form howling in Jealousy" (1.3.36), then "Orc [is] Born then
the Shadowy Female: then All Los's Family" (1.3.40). Plate 4
moves without transition to "the Starry Mills of Satan" which
"are built beneath the Earth & Waters of the Mundane Shell"
(1.4.2-3), and then to Los's address to Satan, his "youngest
born," as Los compares Satan to "Newtons Pantocrator weav-
ing the Woof of Locke" (1.4.11). The plate concludes, bewil-
deringly, with eight lines that have shifted from Los and Satan

---

ton," and James Reiger, " 'The Hems of Their Garments,': The Bard's Song
in *Milton*."

[18] *P & P*, p. 823.

in the fields to "Calvarys foot . . . between South Molton Street & Stratford Place" where modern-day Britons are "preparing for Sacrifice their Cherubim" in ignorance and sadism. Next, Blake gives us the song of the Daughters of Albion as they impose on man the "Moral Virtue [of] the cruel Virgin Babylon" (1.5.27), in an exultation among their "Druid Rocks." This prompts Los to forge "Golgonooza the spiritual Four-fold London eternal," and "loud his Bellows is heard Before London to Hampsteads breadths & Highgates heights"— across all of modern-day London, and on to Mexico, Peru, and beyond. Then begins the substance of the Song as Blake settles into the narrative specifics of Satan who "soft intreated Los to give to him Palamabrons station" (1.7.6).

At first, it may seem that these plates are fragments of some vision arbitrarily flung together. However, if we consider them together we may see that they are an encapsulated history of Blake's own poetry from his Lambeth period to the present—and it should be remembered that all the evidence seems to point to his simultaneous composition of *The Four Zoas*, *Milton*, and *Jerusalem*. More precisely, they are the history of Blake's dawning management of "Voidness," his own previous casting out of Error by giving it form. The cosmogony of plate 3 recapitulates Los-Blake's first fumbling attempts at the creation of mythic order in *The Book of Urizen* and *The Book of Los*, even to the same words and lines; the ensuing births of Orc, the Shadowy Female, and all of Enitharmon's brood recall the Lambeth Prophecies, in which sexual and revolutionary chaos, like Satan here, "Refus[ed] Form." Los confronts Satan in plate 4 of *Milton* quite as if he were the Urizen who had created the Mundane Shell in *The Four Zoas*. Certainly Blake's designation of Satan as "Newtons Pantocrator" is familiar from almost everything else that he wrote, but the Mundane Shell which is created by the "Prince of the Starry Hosts And . . . the Wheels of Heaven" (1.4.9-10) echoes Urizen's desperate attempt to build against the "draught of Voidness" in Night Two of *The Four Zoas*. That represented an advance in Blake's acceptance of disorder, for he had come to see by that time that Urizen's real mistake was to *exclude* "Voidness" from his rotating mandala.

The extended Song of the Daughters of Albion in plate 5 is reminiscent of that of the Females of Amalek in Night Eight of *The Four Zoas* and, to an even greater extent, the similar Daughters in Chapter Three of *Jerusalem*. Also, Blake's strategy in plate 6 of having Los build Golgonooza in London as a reaction to the Daughters' Song is the same that runs throughout *Jerusalem*. As in *Jerusalem* 1.15 and 16 (to cite passages most parallel to the one here in *Milton*), Los extends his vision over contemporary England and builds "the spiritual four-fold London" in weepings and sorrow. Here as there, Blake turns to view chaos as it is manifested all over the world, from "Tyburns Brook" outwards to "the Surrey Hills" to Ireland, and thence to "China and Japan." As Blake knows, "All things begin & end in Albions ancient Druid rocky shore" (1.6.25); and far from being any chauvinist statement, that line relinquishes any border of feeling. It is in this setting, which is within the further frame of the Bard's Song, that Blake is finally able to approach that event at Felpham. He uses art to formalize and fix it for him, with the Song preserved as the opening gate to *Milton*.

Los's sons in the allegory are commonly assigned to different characters in the drama unfolding at Felpham: Satan is the poetaster Hayley, who is trying to usurp the position of genius; Palamabron is the actual Blake at Felpham who was trying to swallow his resentment and placate Hayley; and Rintrah is the internal Blake who finally rose up in "Prophetic Wrath" to assert his true nature no matter what the practical price. But it is Satan's story that actually dominates the Song.

At one level, Satan quite obviously is Hayley, advising Blake on the preferability of miniature painting, engaging him to illustrate small books of verse and ladies' handscreens, frowning at Blake's epic-proportioned poetry. So "Satan with incomparable mildness; His primitive tyrannical attempts on Los: with most endearing love He soft intreated Los to give to him Palamabron's station." Wearied, Los gives him what he wants; nor does Palamabron protest directly to Los, since he "fear'd to be angry lest Satan should accuse him of Ingratitude." What prevails is "Satans mildness and his self-imposition, Seeming a brother, being a tyrant, even thinking himself a brother While he is murdering the just" (1.7.21-23). After Palamabron's horses rage against Satan's guidance, Satan "himself exculpat[ed] with mildest speech. for himself believ'd That he had not opress'd nor injur'd the refractory servants" (1.8.2-3).

But it should be remembered that Satan's chief characteristics are this hypocritical show of friendship *and* his dissimulation of the "fury hidden beneath his own mildness" (1.9.19), which finally flares out before the Assembly in plate 9. It seems apparent that Satan is both Hayley and *also* the persona of Blake himself, with its surface sociability and "correct" idea of what an artist is to be. Hayley may not have been capable of more perceptive behavior at Felpham, but Blake certainly was. Satan's characteristics were Blake's own for too long: the repression of anger in a "soft dissimulation of friendship" as he tried to follow Hayley's bidding. Psychologically, the repression of anger usually leads to depression and a general deadening of *all* feeling as well as the original wrath. "Abstinence sows sand all over The ruddy limbs the flaming hair. . . ." So would not Blake have been slowly turning himself into Hayley as his "heart knock'd against the root of [his] tongue?"[19]

Satan is Blake's persona in another, still more complex way. For the important fact about Satan that Los comes to realize is that Satan is really Urizen in disguise. We have seen in Chapter One how intimately and unmistakably Urizen was the complement of Los, and of Blake the mythmaker as well. As a character, Urizen has changed since Blake's Lambeth period. In those Books, he helped to create the myth—if only by giving negative examples of the possible errors into which the mythmaker may fall. Still, he and Los worked *together* to create

---

[19] Keynes, ed., *Letters of William Blake*, p. 60.

the mythic order that helped Blake to function in the confused British society of the early 1790s. But the situation had changed in many respects by the time that Blake was living at Felpham. Most obviously, it had become apparent to all that the American and French Revolutions were not ushering in the millennium, and that the weary pattern of war and defensive political conservatism was going to continue for a long, long time. But also, by that time Blake had begun to discover the ineradicable darker side of human nature, including his own. Throughout *The Four Zoas*, Urizen kept trying to deny and repress archetypes of the unconscious. He had come to seem like the "social mask" of the mythmaker: only the determined creator of a social and moral order without any room for flaw or weakness, either in himself ("Art thou also become like Vala. thus I cast thee out"—*FZ* 3.43.5) or in others. In the purely personal world of the Bard's Song in *Milton*, he has become simply the collective idea of what the mythmaker should be like.

We should consider a letter that Blake wrote during this period, describing his internal torments: "I labour incessantly & accomplish not one half of what I intend, because my Abstract folly hurries me often away while I am at work, carrying me over Mountains & Valleys, which are not Real, in a Land of Abstraction where Spectres of the Dead wander."[20] When we realize that it was during this time that Blake was gathering together his myth into gigantic epic structures, finally conceptualizing his "System" into consistent form, it is striking that he was so aware of wandering "in a Land of Abstraction." And how like Ulro are those "Mountains & Valleys . . . where Spectres of the Dead wander." The paradox facing the mythmaker that I discussed in Chapter One faces him again here.

A persona is characteristically dominated by the psychological function (Thinking, Feeling, Intuition, or Sensation) that controls the conscious personality. Both Hayley and Urizen seem dominated by the Thinking function, one in an extra-

[20] *Ibid.*, p. 51.

verted and one in an introverted way. Jung describes this func-
tion according to the type of person: "As a consequence of . . .
extraversion . . . thinking is oriented by the object and objec-
tive data. . . . For the extraverted judgment, the criterion
supplied by external conditions is the valid and determining
one . . . the ideas it operates with are largely borrowed from
outside, i.e., have been transmitted by tradition and educa-
tion."[21] Introverted thinking is "directed to subjective ideas
or subjective facts,"[22] and it wants "to see how the external
fact will fit into . . . the framework of the idea."[23] It "shows a
dangerous tendency to force the facts into the shape of its im-
age," and "it creates theories for their own sake."[24]

Reasonable and rational Hayley seems to have been inaltera-
bly one with what he was expected to be by his "tradition and
education." All of the evidence shows that he considered him-
self an accomplished poet worthy of emulation, a luminary of
his country society, a generous patron of artists who unfortu-
nately came to naught (like Romney and Blake), and generally
a noble fellow. Urizen's besetting error, which Blake always
saw, was exactly that he kept trying to "coerce facts for the
sake of theories." Originally creating form for the "shapes
Bred from his forsaken wilderness" (*BU* 1.3.14-15), Urizen
goes on trying to impose "one Law" in different ways from *The
Book of Urizen* onwards. And Blake quite consciously assigned
the thinking "faculty" to Urizen in *The Four Zoas*.

However, the Bard's Song represents more than Blake's
growing awareness of his persona which must be "dissolved,"
for in it he comes to terms with his Shadow side as well.
Blake's behavior at Felpham showed this Shadow quite clearly,
for it included all of the characteristics that Blake had most
attacked in his previous poetry. To begin with, he suppressed
his rage for a long time, with just the results predicted in "The
Poison Tree" of *The Songs of Experience*. He had also been dis-
honest both with himself and with Hayley, using "blandish-
ments" to get his way. (Blake wrote in his private Notebook:

[21] Jung, *Psychological Types*, p. 342.   [22] *Ibid.*, p. 344.
[23] *Ibid.*, p. 381.   [24] *Ibid.*

"To H— the Pick thank. I write the Rascal Thanks till he & I
With Thanks & Compliments are quite drawn dry." But it is
impossible to be hard on Blake here, considering the realities
of the situation.) And for too many years at Felpham, Blake
had done the very worst thing: he had let his concern for his
own material welfare come before his concern for the welfare of
"Albion" as he attempted to hide his epic talents. Los's own
Shadow, or Spectre, was to worry him on this point again in
the beginning of *Jerusalem*, when he taunted Los about Los's
unceasing love for Albion:

> . . . Wilt thou still go on to destruction?
> Till thy life is all taken away by this deceitful Friendship?
> He drinks thee up like water! like wine he pours thee . . .
>
> *(J* 1.7.9-11)

Blake himself had grown "Opake to the Divine Vision" of the
sacrificial Christ.

What is so remarkable about the Bard's Song is its revela-
tion of Blake's degree of self-insight. For during the Song he is
becoming conscious of his act of projecting onto "evil" others
his *own* qualities. Satan is, after all, one of Los's sons, and if he
obviously represents Hayley, then Hayley in turn represents
some part of Los . . . and Blake. Los really proves as culpable as
Satan, for he hid his wrath toward Satan, and could not judge
to put him in his place, thus causing more confusion than
ever. The point I would make is that Blake's very construction
of the allegory here suggests that he is "incorporating his
Shadow," as Jung would have it. And indeed, Urizen is never
very prominent again. He appears briefly to pour ice water on
Milton's overheated brain later in Book One (not necessarily a
bad idea); he is merely one of Albion's Zoas in plate 40 of Book
Two; he does not figure at all in *Jerusalem*. Nor do Milton or
Blake in *Milton*, or Los in *Jerusalem*, ever again shrink from the
"Mental Fight" to "buil[d] Jerusalem In England's green &
pleasant land" (1.1.15-16).

Satan's own "flaming with Rintrahs fury hidden beneath his
own mildness" (1.9.19) helps to burn away Error in the poem.

What he makes possible ultimately is the exploration of "the Abyss," or the unconscious, with which the rest of the poem is concerned. Satan is closely connected to Ulro, as Jung says the Shadow is with the personal unconscious, and when he reveals his true nature, all at the Assembly discover corresponding darknesses. Satan "grew Opake against the Divine Vision" and in his bosom opens the "World of deeper Ulro" which is "a vast unfathomable Abyss" (1.9.30-35). The others at the Assembly are covered in terrible darkness, Satan "triumphant divide[s] the Nations," and (as Los laments) "Jealousy run[s] along the mountains" (1.10.14). But no one in the Assembly previous to Satan's sudden unveiling seemed to have much comprehension of Ulro or the "vast Abyss" lying all around them, and they are rather like the sheltered innocents in *The Book of Thel* and *Tiriel*. Since they had no real knowledge of it, they were quite fooled by exterior appearances and unable to judge Error when it came before them. Their true nature is revealed at the end of the Bard's Song, for (unlike the Seven Eyes of God in *The Four Zoas* and the Divine Family in *Jerusalem*) they are a failed mandala, with each member refusing its archetypal function of unification:

> Triple Elohim came: Elohim wearied fainted: they elected
> Shaddai.
> Shaddai angry, Pahad descended: Pahad terrified, they sent
> Jehovah
> And Jehovah was leprous . . .
>
> (1.13.22-24)

So *they* have disguised their own answering correspondence to Satan's Ulro as they sat "at eternal tables" listening to the Bard.

Further, unless this "vast Abyss" (with which no one seems reconciled) had been opened to the gaze of all, Milton could never have been reunited with his "Sixfold Emanation scatter'd thro' the deep" (1.2.19). Nor could Blake the Bard himself (living in the present unredeemed society of Britain) have sung the terrors of Ulro, which he saw about him on "Albions . . .

rocky shore," terrors to be brought before the contemplative thoughts of the readers of the rest of *Milton* and *Jerusalem*. Anger must be let out everywhere to cleanse.

This revelation of the actual Ulro which has been concealed in Satan's inner nature purges at least Blake of his own satanic nature in the Felpham incident. For after Satan shows his "fury hidden beneath his own mildness," the effects run everywhere through the cartography of Blake's myth and that particular Error of behavior becomes dross that must be cast off. For how can Blake again act as he did at Felpham (concealing his genius as well as his rage) if that psychological error causes Satan to "s[i]nk down [in] a dreadful Death, unlike the slumbers of Beulah," and "his Spectre raging furious descended into its Space . . . Drawn down by Orc & the Shadowy Female into Generation," followed by "Enitharmon [who] enterd weeping into the Space," eventually "closing Los from Eternity in Albions cliffs" and causing "Satans Druid sons [to] Offer the Human Victims throughout all the earth" (1.9.48-11.8)?

It is after achieving such self-knowledge that Blake turns to analyze Hayley's own dull (because incapable of change) behavior in the situation, due in large part to Hayley's particularly obtuse relationship with his own unconscious. That is, Hayley's "Error" was due to his "Blockhead" nature (as Blake characterized many of his corporeal friends—including Hayley—in his Notebook) and not to any vastly more sinister participation in "the Abysses of the Accuser."[25] Leutha's long speech in plate 12 reveals that Satan has all along been a man "possessed by his anima," as Jung would say, with his "soft dissimulation of friendship" and "blandishments" quite like those of Leutha toward all around her. Such "possession" usually takes place only when one will not give the unconscious its due: such as when one lives in complete accordance with one's persona. Jung describes the relationship between persona and anima well. "Outwardly [the man] plays the strong man . . . he becomes inwardly a woman, i.e., the anima, for it is the

[25] Keynes, ed., *Letters of William Blake*, p. 59.

anima that reacts to the persona . . . because a man is all the less capable of conceiving his weaknesses the more he is identified with the persona, the persona's counterpart, the anima . . . is at once projected."[26]

It seems clear from internal evidence that the Satan of plate 12 is Hayley alone. Echoes of the Notebook run through Leutha's speech. When she says of her conduct:

> To do unkind things in kindness! with power armd, to say
> The most irritating things in the midst of tears and love
> These are the stings of the Serpent! thus did we by them; till thus
> They in return retaliated, and the Living Creatures maddend
> (I.12.32-35)

her language is reminiscent of these lines from the Notebook:

> When H——y finds out what you cannot do
> That is the very thing hell set you to

Or

> To H——
> Thy Friendship oft has made my heart to ake
> Do be my Enemy for Friendships sake.

There is also the parallel between Blake's acid couplet:

> Of H s birth this was the happy lot
> His Mother on his Father him begot

and the lines spoken by Leutha:

> Like sweet perfumes I stupified the masculine perceptions
> And kept only the feminine awake . . .
> (I.12.5-6)

Both passages have been taken to mean that Blake was accusing Hayley of being a repressed homosexual, especially since the lines from *Milton* continue:

[26] Jung, *Two Essays*, pp. 194-95.

. . . hence rose his soft
Delusory love to Palamabron: admiration join'd with envy
Cupidity unconquerable!

(1.12.6-7)

Perhaps so, but I think that the reality was both subtler and
more far-reaching than that, and that these lines rather refer to
the way in which Hayley's own projections have fastened onto
Blake. The situation is better comprehended if we consider
that the anima is very close to the unconscious, and is seen
either negatively or positively according to the way in which
the man views the unconscious.

For everything "bad" that Satan has done is faulted to
Leutha, and all of it suggests the overwhelming influence of
the unconscious. When the horses would rest at noon, she
"sprang out of the breast of Satan" and unloosed them; they
broke their controlling reins, "terribly rag[ing]." Satan feebly
tried to control them in "banks of sand . . . in labyrinthine
forms" with predictable results: "the Harrow cast thick flames:
Jehovah thunderd above." The flames of Hell comprise her
"moth-like elegance" which so captivates the Assembly, as it
did Satan and Los's Gnomes. It is with these "dark fires Which
now gird round us" that she "form'd the Serpent Of precious
stones & gold turn'd poisons on the sultry wastes"—yet
another rising sexual serpent like Vala in Luvah's description
in Night Two of *The Four Zoas*. And as day closes, Leutha re-
treats back "in Satan's inmost brain," for in the night to come
her maddening influence will not be needed: Satan becomes
"wild with prophetic fury his former life bec[o]me[s] like a
dream Cloth'd in the Serpents folds, in selfish holiness de-
manding purity Being most impure" (1.12.45-47).

The Bard's Song ends after the Assembly has been con-
founded, Satan revealed, the "Seven Eyes" proven blind,
Leutha's daughters Rahab and Tirzah born, and all present left
weltering in their particular versions of Ulro. And this Song,
declares the Bard, is "according to the inspiration of the Poetic
Genius Who is the eternal all-protecting Divine Humanity"
(1.14.1-2): all included as part of the greater totality of the

Self, in other words. The "great murmuring . . . in doubtfulness" of the purely circumstantial world of "Albion" now caught in the historical troubles of "Italy Greece & Egypt To Tartary & Hindostan & China & to Great America" will not disperse the Bard's new insight: the social prophet must continue his journey into the deeper Self if he is to regenerate Albion. And so "the loud voic'd Bard terrify'd took refuge in Miltons bosom" (1.14.9).

Jung trenchantly analyzes the dangers present for the conscious ego that has begun to reach some knowledge of the unconscious, which was Blake's own situation as he worked with *The Four Zoas* and *Milton*. The greatest danger in *Milton* is that Blake will become possessed by those archetypes from the unconscious with which he has become familiar: schizophrenia. Either he will see himself as the literal reincarnation of Milton with all of the great power associated with that culture hero; or he will be engulfed by archetypes, hearing and seeing Milton and Los as objective realities which he will no longer be able to use for his own conscious mythic purposes.

The unconscious possesses great mana (as Jung terms it). When the conscious ego begins to comprehend the unconscious, the great temptation is for the ego to assume that it now knows everything: that it now has the mana previously belonging to the unconscious. In Jung's words, "thus the ego becomes a mana-personality. But the mana-personality is a dominant of the collective unconscious. . . . This masculine collective figure" (which the patient believes is *himself*) entails the psychic danger of inflation, "for by inflating the conscious mind it can destroy everything that was gained by coming to terms with the [personal unconscious]. . . . The ego has appropriated something that does not belong to it."[27]

Ironically enough, this psychic inflation, which has been caused by the new familiarity with the unconscious, makes the unconscious attack consciousness in new form. This happens "infallibly . . . if the conscious attitude has a flaw in it. . . . If the ego presumes to wield power over the unconscious, the un-

[27] *Ibid.*, pp. 228-29.

conscious reacts . . . [by] deploying the dominant of the
mana-personality. . . . Against this the only defence is full
confession of one's weakness in face of the powers of the uncon-
scious. By opposing no force to the unconscious we do not
provoke it to attack."[28]

So the reason why it was so important for Blake to preserve
the Bard's Song as a kind of prelude to the poem proper is that
it is a memorial of his own weaknesses that may so easily reoc-
cur. That Song remains permanently as part of *Milton*; and
while many critics see it as an allegory of Blake's proud victory
over his adversary Hayley, I see it as an allegory of Blake's
metamorphosis into Hayley and his abandonment of Albion. It
is not part of the past that may be discarded, for "mark well
my words! they are your eternal salvation," as the Bard repeats
again and again during his Song. What insight Blake does
gain afterwards is gotten "in Miltons bosom," and the mana
clearly belongs to the archetypal figure of Milton. Blake at the
very end of the poem is Blake acting on the wisdom passed to
him by Milton, still living in the setting that originally re-
vealed his own "Opakeness" and not at all the godlike cultural
hero.

Milton himself seems to act as the Wise Old Man archetype
in the poem, and his presence suggests both that Blake has
reached the stage in his psychological development which is
very close to reunification (or "regeneration"), and that Blake
is approaching the unconscious with that attitude of accept-
ance which was discussed in Chapters Two and Three. Blake
descends into "Eternal Death" much as Dante did into Purga-
tory and Hell, relying upon the guidance of a master. Blake
makes the trip by himself once more in *Jerusalem*, finally at its
end hearing Albion's continual process of "living, going forth
& returning wearied" as Blake "repos[es] And then Awak[ens]
into [Jesus'] Bosom" (*J* 4.99.3-4). Here in *Milton*, the arche-
type that completes the quaternity of male wholeness is
needed.

The archetype itself represents the spirit in the form of a

[28] *Ibid.*, p. 234.

man possessing great authority, appearing in situations requiring great insight and determination that cannot be mustered by the person to whom the archetype appears.[29] "Often [he] asks questions like who? why? whence? . . . for the purpose of inducing self-reflection and mobilizing the moral forces, and . . . bring[s] knowledge of the immediate situation as well as of the goal." This archetype "represents knowledge . . . insight, wisdom, and . . . moral qualities . . . which make his 'spiritual' character sufficiently plain."[30]

One should note the change in the nature of chaos as it appears in *Milton* from what it seemed in *The Four Zoas*: here, it is specific, political, and involving. This immediate rendering only really appeared in Night Eight of *The Four Zoas*, and then briefly. *Jerusalem* will be concerned throughout 93 of its 100 plates with these social manifestations of man's inner darkness, exploring it as fully as Blake can manage. One reason that the poem *Milton* is important to any understanding of Blake is because it is a kind of waystation in this voyage to the interior. Milton as an historical figure given archetypal proportions was a political prophet, a genuine culture hero who was also a brilliant poet, and it seems clear that Blake felt that social disorder could only be faced (at least initially) in his presence. That is, Blake's individual conscious ego needed the mana of the collective unconscious to deal with the negative side of the unconscious *for the good of Albion*. And Milton-Blake's descent into "Eternal Death" is followed by the concluding nine plates of Book One giving us "the World of Los . . . a Vision of the Science of the Elohim" (1.29.64-65): non-myth again answered by myth.

After the Bard has finished his Song, Milton begins his journey downward by asking questions:

When will the Resurrection come; to deliver the sleeping body
From corruptibility: O when Lord Jesus wilt thou come?
. . .

---

[29] Jung, *Archetypes*, p. 217.   [30] *Ibid.*, pp. 220, 222.

> What do I here before the Judgment? without my
>   Emanation?
> With the daughters of memory, & not with the daughters of
>   inspiration[?]

(1.14.17-18 and 28-29)

Milton's answer is to descend to "look forth for the morning of
the grave" (1.14.20), not at all the Zoas' forced falls, which
were accompanied by terror. He realizes, as Blake just has in
the course of the Song, that "I in my Selfhood am that Satan: I
am that Evil One!" (1.14.30); further, that what he must do is
to separate Satan "from my Hells" . . . those Hells themselves
being, as Milton understands, "*my* Furnaces" [italics added].

It is at this point that Blake enters as one character among
many, making us aware of his twofold nature in the poem:
both the Blake who experienced "possession" by the mana of
Milton in the recent past and the Blake who lives in "Albions
land: Which is this earth of vegetation on which now I write"
(1.14.40-41). As I said before, Blake himself invites us to read
the poem as a document of a psychological process which yet is
becoming art before our eyes. Just before Milton enters Blake's
foot, Milton sees Albion near death "upon the Rock of Ages,"
and so when he does fuse his vision with Blake's that terrible
sight of the dissolving body politic becomes Blake's as well. In
the next four plates, the two see the terrible social realities of
"Albions heart" (1.20.41), much as Los sees the "Minute Par-
ticulars of Albion" when he takes "his globe of fire to search
the interiors of Albions bosom" in Chapter Two of *Jerusalem*.
There are "the Cruelties of Ulro": "the sick Father & his starv-
ing Family!"; "the Prisoner in the stone Dungeon & the Slave
at the Mill"; the oppressing "Kings," "Councellors & Mighty
Men"; "Pestilence," "Famine," and "War" (1.18.10-17).

Near the end of this journey through Albion's heart, Milton
meets Urizen. Each benefits the other here, even though "the
Man and Demon strove many periods" (1.19.27), for:

> . . . with cold hand Urizen stoop'd down
> And took up water from the river Jordan: pouring on

To Miltons brain the icy fluid from his broad cold palm
But Milton took of the red clay of Succoth, moulding it
   with care . . .
Creating new flesh on the Demon cold . . .

(1.19.7-13)

Bloom sees Urizen's activity here as another attempt to bind
man by moral law,[31] which may be so (Milton tried to ap-
proach "the Universe of Los and Enitharmon . . . but Urizen
oppos'd his path"—1.19.25-26); however, one should remem-
ber the horrors which Milton has been viewing, and contrast
Los's own reaction to similar sights in Chapter Three of
Jerusalem, where *he* nearly lost control:

  And Los shouted with ceaseless shoutings & his tears
    poured down
  His immortal cheeks, rearing his hands to heaven for aid
    Divine!

(*J* 3.71.56-57)

It seems more that Urizen proves necessary for Milton here, as
he did for Los long ago in the Lambeth Books.

Blake again enters the poem, after the final chant of Rahab
and Tirzah, which recollects the Song of the Females of
Amalek in Night Eight of *The Four Zoas* in its glorification of
the cruelties of war and "Natural Religion." Here again we
have one of those startling jumps in perspective that were so
common in the Bard's Song. But it can only be Blake here,
since he speaks of "the Spectrous body of Milton Redounding
from my left foot into Los's Mundane space" (1.20.20-21), and
the passage following Albion's beginning "turn[ing] upon his
Couch" (1.20.25) is Blake's familiar message that "Everything
that lives is holy." This passage is what Blake has learned from
all of the events so far (those of the Bard's Song as well as Mil-
ton's descent into "Eternal Death"), spoken in spite of the so-
cial confusion that has just been seen: everything may open
outward (and inward) to include the world, heaven, and hell,

---

[31] *P & P*, p. 831.

as these dimensions of existence are to be found everywhere.

> Seest thou the little winged fly, smaller than a grain of
>   sand?
> It has a heart like thee; a brain open to heaven & hell . . .
> Seek not thy heavenly father then beyond the skies:
> There Chaos dwells & ancient Night & Og & Anak old:
> For every human heart has gates of brass & bars of adamant,
> Which few dare unbar because dread Og & Anak guard the
>   gates . . .
> . . . for in brain and heart and loins
> Gates open behind Satans Seat to the City of Golgonooza
> Which is the spiritual fourfold London, in the loins of
>   Albion.

> > (1.20.27-40)

God dwells within man's heart and brain as well as "up there"—not a startlingly new theological conception. But Satan dwells there too, for by implication he is not to be found "beyond the skies" any more than is "the heavenly father." "Satans Seat" is near these gates of the heart; although the further that one penetrates within, the closer one comes to "the City of Golgonooza Which is the spiritual fourfold London" in, literally enough, the center of man—"in the loins of Albion." Creation *itself* needs hell as well as heaven.

Then "Milton fell thro Albions heart, travelling outside of Humanity Beyond the Stars in Chaos" (1.20.41-42), and enters Blake's left foot (the left side has always been a symbol of the unconscious)—and that is the last we see of Milton for the rest of Book One. The character Blake takes over the nine plates that are left, still in the beginning under the influence of Milton, though fast becoming his own man. His first act is to see for himself what Milton saw:

> But Milton entering my Foot; I saw in the nether
> Regions of the Imagination; also all men on Earth,
> And all in Heaven, saw in the nether reaches of the
>   Imagination
> In Ulro beneath Beulah, the vast breach of Miltons descent.

> > (1.21.4-7)

And that is not all: Los comes to Blake as well, so that the three merge with Blake's individuality triumphant in the end at "Felphams Vale." Schizophrenia seems especially possible with the presence of Los. I am *not* trying to say that Blake himself was on the brink of schizophrenia at Felpham, only that the situation in the poem is at this point analogous to the clinical one. Blake avoids disintegration in the poem as Jung suggests the individual does: through constant awareness that the limited conscious ego may learn from the archetypes about the unconscious, but should not assume their grandeur. Here, Blake gives us his own "Divine Vision" only in the company of Milton and Los; in *Jerusalem*, only in the guise of Los (save, it is true, for those startling final four plates).

Blake's "possession" (1.22.14) by Los is emphasized, and Blake does not appear again as a character until Ololon enters his cottage at Felpham in plate 36 of Book Two, and we are back again in the limited time of the present.

> . . . *we* went along to [Los's] supreme abode
> Rintrah and Palamabron met *us* at the Gate of Golgonooza
> Clouded with discontent. & brooding in their minds
>   terrible things . . . [italics added]
>   (1.22.26-28)

Their fear is Blake's old one: if the poet-prophet really enters into the nature of the Ulro all around him, he will "become what he beholds." Milton, say Rintrah and Palamabron,

> Will unchain Orc[,] & let loose Satan, Og, Sihon, & Anak
> Upon the Body of Albion . . .
> The Daughters of Los . . .
> . . . weave a new Religion from new Jealousy of
>   Theotormon!
> Miltons Religion is the cause: there is no end to destruction!
>   . . .
> Milton will utterly consume us & thee our beloved Father[.]
> He hath enterd into the Covering Cherub . . .
>   (1.22.33-39, 23.13-14)

But Los gives them the new answer that Blake has been learning: one may "become what one beholds"—in fact, one should in order to maintain one's humility—and still in that empathy *resist* the underlying principle that one beholds.

> I have embracd the falling Death, he is become One with
>   me
> O Sons we live not by wrath. by mercy alone we live!
> . . . O go not forth in Martyrdoms & Wars
> We were plac'd here by the Universal Brotherhood & Mercy
>   . . .
> Till Albion is arisen; then patient wait a little while . . .
> Arise O Sons give all your strength against Eternal Death
>   . . .
>
>   (I.23.33-34, 23.49-54, 24.34)

And for the rest of Book One, Los and his Sons do use "all [their] strength against Eternal Death," for they labor like artists to give mythic order to all of the disorder around them. Eternity is more usually seen as larger than large; here, it is smaller than small and everything closes inward to open magically into "the heavens of bright eternity" (I.28.38). This is the general psychological movement in the poem as well, thus justifying Blake's inquiry into his relations with Hayley and his experiences in "Felphams Vale." Here, Los and his Sons are busy creating a true mandala in their City, which is made out of the materials at hand—Law, man's physical body, War, Commerce, Industry, Time, and Space: the archetype in art thus enabling the reader as well as the poet to look at the Ulro all around him without "becom[ing] what he beholds."

Los creates Bowlahoola "namd Law" on his "Anvils" and "furnaces [which] rage," and Bloom notes disapprovingly that this "grotesque passage" cannot really be "excuse[d]."[32] But Blake's portrayal of man's alimentary, digestive, and excrementatory tracts is as exuberantly and vulgarly funny as anything he has written—why should not this have a place in "the World of Los" as well as everything else?

[32] *Ibid.*, p. 834.

The Furnaces the Stomach for digestion. terrible their fury

. . .

The double drum drowns howls & groans, the shrill fife.
    shrieks & cries
The crooked horn mellows the hoarse raving serpent,
    terrible but harmonious
Bowlahoola is the Stomach in every individual man.

(1.24.59-67)

Los gathers all men together for the Vintage and Harvest to
come, separating them into the "Three Classes" (the Elect, the
Reprobate, and the Redeemed), grinding, crushing all of them
in preparation. Blake's metaphor changes here from what it
was in Night Nine of *The Four Zoas*. There, such sufferings as
were known by men were part of an ongoing process which was
accomplished in the poetic form. Here, these torments are not
really apocalyptic (not being part of the "Last Days"), but
examples of the social Ulro to which Los is giving meaning.
"The Wine-press of Los," in which the sons and daughters of
Los tread the grapes and around which the creatures of the
earth dance, now "is call'd War on Earth, it is the Printing-
Press Of Los" (1.27.8-9). This "Wine-press" is "eastward of
Golgonooza" (1.27.1). "The Cultivated land" around Gol-
gonooza is "Allamanda calld on Earth Commerce" (1.27.42),
and here are to be seen "the Mills of Theotormon" and "the
starry voids" of the natural world ("oceans, clouds & waters,"
"the Sun & Moon"). The natural sciences become part of the
scene too, being the manifestations "in Time & Space" of "the
four Arts" even though they are limited versions of the real
thing, "shut out" (1.27.57).

The Sons of Los work with psychological materials also:

Creating form & beauty around the dark regions of sorrow

. . .

Creating the beautiful House for the piteous sufferer.
Others; Cabinets richly fabricate of gold & ivory;
For Doubts & fears unform'd & wretched & melancholy.

(1.28.2-9)

Other Sons work with Time, building the permanent form of their "City" with its walls and gates, terraces, towers, and bridged moats; all of this time collapsed into one interior moment "less than a pulsation of the artery" (I.28.62). Space is likewise transformed by the Sons, everything shrunk (but expanded at the same time) to the "neighborhood" of the individual man. This passage (I.29.4-14) involves the reader too, as did Blake's description of the human body in *The Book of Urizen*, for it is exactly the way we have all seen things without knowing their archetypal significance:

> . . . every Space that a Man views around his
>   dwelling-place:
> Standing on his own roof, or in his garden on a mount
> Of twenty-five cubits in height, such space is his Universe;
> And on its verge the Sun rises & sets. the Clouds bow
> To meet the flat Earth & the Sea in such an orderd Space
>   (I.29.4-9)

Man's senses are relegated to the Zoas and so given their form according to the myth; Rahab and Tirzah "weave [their] black Woof of Death" (in the British mills of industry, presumably), and "the stamping feet of Zelophehads Daughters are coverd with Human gore" (from British wars)—but meanwhile around them walk "the Seven Eyes of God" and they are washed by "the River . . . [which] takes [the Woof] in his arms" in an apparently perpetual baptism into the spirit. In this grand culmination to Book One which has made "Nature [into] a Vision of the Science of the Elohim" (I.29.65), everything fallen is given its place in the myth.

Albion as a type of Adam Kadmon must represent both male and female experience, and Blake learns the nature of Albion's dissolution both from the masculine and the feminine points of view. If Book One was Milton's book, Book Two is Ololon's (at least during the descent through the heavens to Felpham, or until II.35.47). "Pity must join together those whom wrath has torn in sunder" (*J* 1.7.62). In many ways, the plates of

Book Two that have to do with Ololon parallel those of Book One that have to do with Milton.

She is a powerful and positive anima figure both for Milton and Blake, and reunion with her (as Blake sees under Milton's aegis) is quite necessary "before the Judgment" (I. 14.28) which will be Regeneration. We have already seen the negative side of the anima in the figure of Leutha, Satan's unacknowledged "feminine" side, which controls his behavior so that he uses her tricks of "soft blandishments" and moody weeping to get his way with Los in the Bard's Song. Ololon shows what an anima may do for a man if he takes a positive approach to that which Satan fears, and certainly Milton does that. So does Blake, if we consider that in these opening plates to Book Two he shares the archetypal feminine perception of existence.

The opening two plates of Book Two give us Beulah, and we join the peaceful inhabitants of that place as fully as we did the more strenuous Sons of Los in the immediately preceding plates. The Sons of Eden need Beulah's "moony shades and hills" as much as the Emanations there need the Sons' fiery imaginations which create for them "a habitation & a place" (II. 30.24), and also the Sons' vigorous "joy" (II. 30.23). Many critics have mentioned the essentially maternal quality of Beulah, and indeed Blake here compares the inhabitants of Beulah to "the beloved infant in his mothers bosom round incircled With arms of love & pity & sweet compassion" (II. 30. 11-12). But there is a more profound quality to Beulah (which means "married" in Hebrew). Jung captures its essence in his essay, "Marriage as a Psychological Relationship."[33] Marriage usually begins in "non-differentiation," in that each presupposes in the other a psychological state similar to his/her own. Sexuality supports this feeling, creating as it does the feeling of complete harmony "since the return to that original condition of unconscious oneness is like a return to childhood . . . even more . . . a return to the mother's womb."[34] The crisis in a marriage comes, Jung thinks, when both become

[33] Jung, *The Development of Personality*, p. 187.   [34] *Ibid.*, p. 192.

aware that this is not the real situation and have to come to terms with each other's psychological differences. That state of "non-differentiation" sounds very close to Beulah, for the trouble with Beulah is that if one stays there too long ("married" to it either as a resting Son of Eden or an Emanation who cannot somehow take on to herself the Sons' energy) one turns into the undifferentiated Other, lost in the womb once more.

But at its best, Beulah creates in its inhabitants a yearning and compassionate sympathy for everything that lives, exactly the way that a mother feels for all other children that she sees. So in "the Lamentation of Beulah" in plate 31, the lark that sings with "his little throat labour[ing] with inspiration" and every tiny feather "vibrat[ing] with the effluence Divine" makes "all Nature listen silent to him & the awful Sun Stands still upon the Mountain"—like parents marveling at their child. The same is true of the flowers that "put forth their precious Odours! And none can tell how from so small a center comes such sweets" (II.31.46-47). All of the humble flowers of English gardens and meadows unite "all in order sweet & lovely" and "Men are sick with Love!" (II.31.62). Is that "Love" romantic eros, or is it a more universal empathy for those "Tree[s] and Flower[s] & Herb[s]"? Probably both—one leads to the other, evidently.

Blake had opened Book One with the command to the Daughters of Beulah to "record the journey of immortal Milton thro' your realms," himself thus a Son of Eden needing Beulah; this beginning of Book Two makes it clear that Blake now enters those realms too as he had not before. How exclusively male in creation and operation that Golgonooza at the end of Book One seems! Everything is "fabricate[d]" and cleverly wrought, but there is not the same intuitive warmth felt toward the elements of Golgonooza by its creators as there is by the Daughters toward this "little bird" which causes even the "awful Sun" to look upon it "with eyes of soft humility, & wonder love & awe" (II.31.38).

There is a further "Song of Beulah" here, which indicates that the other aspect of the archetypal Feminine is being approached, dealing as it does with the state of Jealousy. "The soft dissimulation of friendship" in the Bard's Song was the repression of wrath in the name of duty; jealousy here is repression of sexuality for the same reason. That "dissimulation" turned aside the wrath of Palamabron, Los, and most especially Satan himself so that all assumed the same limply smiling appearance, and the unmasking of the true emotion was essential to the beginning of Milton's descent. Here too, in plate 33, Christ addresses the "Daughters of Babylon": her jealousy "cut[s] off my loves in fury till I have no love left for thee" (II.33.7), and the "Female" sees that "all his loves by her cut off: he leaves Her also: intirely abstracting himself from Female loves" (II.33.15-16). This is the other side of Beulah. Beulah (which, according to II.32.33, may become a State if divorced from Imagination) and Jealousy both are inward-directed, always trying to preserve by holding on. What is being curbed through duty is "the Divine Voice," another abandonment of the "Divine Vision" like that which was known by Blake in the Bard's Song. Here there is the "Daughter's" selfish desire to keep the vision to herself; and we should remember how consistently in Blake's works fulfilled sexuality expands characters' perceptions outwards to affect the whole world.

When Satan's wrath was finally loosed upon the Assembly, and Los's flared up to answer it, Milton was finally able to begin his descent through Ulro. In this plate, the "Female":

. . . relent[s] in fear of death: She shall begin to give
Her maidens to her husband: delighting in his delight
And then & then alone begins the happy Female joy
As it is done in Beulah.

                                                        (II.33.17-20)

And Ololon begins to descend through Or-Ulro.

Blake entered "Albions heart" with Milton in Book One to explore the Ulro there. It proved to be a hard, rocky, arid place whose political correspondences were warfare, monarchy, and imperialism—all masculine tyrannies. In plates 17 and 18,

Milton "continu'd journeying above The rocky masses of The Mundane Shell," and sees "the Cruelties of Ulro": "Kings . . . & Councellors & Mighty Men . . . the Pestilence . . . its fringe & the War its girdle . . . Holiness [put on] as a breastplate & as a helmet" (I. 18. 15-21). But Ololon's Ulro is:

> . . . a vast Polypus
> Of living fibres down into the Sea of Time & Space growing
> A self-devouring monstous Human Death Twenty-seven
>   fold[.]
> Within it sit Five Females & the nameless
>   Shadowy Mother
> Spinning it from their bowels with songs of amorous
>   delight.
>
> (II.34.24-28)

Here we can see all of the chthonic archetypal characteristics of the Feminine: the genitalia that suffocate—and by implication castrate—everything that enters ("a vast Polypus Of living fibres down into the Sea of Time & Space"), the maternal womb that produces life but then refuses to let that life break away into independence ("a self-devouring monstrous Human Death . . . the nameless Shadowy Mother"), what Jung calls "her orgiastic [sic] emotionality"[35] which is as anonymous as it is involving ("spinning it from their bowels with songs of amorous delight").

The social manifestations of that Or-Ulro are equally feminine in connotation, for what Ololon sees as she descends are not war and imperialism but the contemporary textile mills, usually feminine in association for Blake. (Albion, Samson, and Milton may "labour at the mill with slaves," but they are there to share the workers' lot rather than become slaves themselves.) As Blake writes in *Jerusalem*, "The Male is a Furnace of beryll; the Female is a golden Loom" (*J* 1.5.34). So Ololon sees the "dreadful Loom of Death" with "piteous Female forms compelld To weave the Woof of Death . . . to Blackheath the dark Woof! Loud Loud roll the Weights &

[35] Jung, *Archetypes*, p. 82.

Spindles over the whole Earth" (II.35.7-14). The passage through Ulro and immersion in its contemporary manifestations had been necessary for Ololon as well. As Blake emphasizes:

> . . . they
> Could not behold Golgonooza without passing the
>   Polypus . . .
> For Golgonooza cannot be seen till having passd the
>   Polypus
>
> (II.35.18-22)

And since we know from plate 32 that Milton is "on the Couch of Death," to find him she must "examine all the Couches of the Dead" on which lie "all the Sons of Albion" (II.35.26-27). She finds Milton in the "midst of these," and finally descends "thro Beulah to Los & Enitharmon," and through them to the waiting William Blake. So her last sight before breaking through the veil of myth into the present is *of* the present in its most confused social form.

Both descents through Ulro over, that dark territory is now known from the contrary viewpoints of Milton and Ololon; and this is when Ololon appears in Blake's garden and we return to the present. That moment has the previous experiences bearing upon it, however, and everything in the concluding plates of the poem is charged with archetypal energy. In this moment when Ololon is about to descend into Blake's garden, the wild thyme and lark which we have met earlier in the gentle visions of Beulah have been transfigured into images of the Self: wrath finally joined to pity. "The Wild Thyme" that had been one of many "Odours" that were "downy & soft waving among the reeds" (II.31.52) is now "a mighty Demon" which, though "Los's Messenger to Eden," penetrates down to Ulro where he seems "terrible deadly & poisonous" (II.35.54-55). The lark that had been "this little Bird" (II.31.37) is now become "a mighty Angel" and "Messenger" from the heavens, as he had been in Book One: a symbol of the outward boundary of the Mundane Shell, "Chaos And Ancient Night; & Purgatory"

(I.17.24-25). Yet the local quality is preserved, as it is throughout these final nine plates. Blake's separation from Milton is important here, for he is at last able to face these archetypes (appearing in negative and positive forms) without an intermediary. Part of that separation is implied by the specificity of these symbols, savored in their particulars. So the thyme is both "a mighty Demon . . . dark" and a "small Root creeping in grass"; and the larks that "all night consult with Angels of Providence & with the Eyes of God" also meet other larks "& back to back They touch their pinions tip tip" (II.36.2-5). Ololon is invited by Blake to enter his "Cottage" and comfort his "Shadow of Delight" who "is sick with fatigue": Catherine, who had been laboring at the engraver's press along with Blake.

These plates also see Blake gradually reducing the archetypal stature of Milton, seeing for the first time in the poem Milton's own "Error."

> I beheld Milton with astonishment & in him beheld
> The Monstrous Churches of Beulah, the Gods of Ulro dark.
> (II.37.15-16)

The names of these Churches and Gods follow, all belonging to institutionalized religions. As Bloom notes, "Milton's Shadow consists of the errors of vision in his work, and the consequent influence of those errors on English culture."[36] This "Shadow" also turns out to be the error of the overly systematic mythmaker that Blake himself knew so well, and had had to "annihilate" in his own way. When Milton does at last come down "out from the eastern sky . . . descending down into my Cottage Garden," he does so in the historic garb of the Puritan ("clothed in black, severe & silent") which disturbingly echoes the "Priests in black gowns . . . binding with briars . . . joys & desires" (S. of E., "The Garden of Love").

Blake says, "I saw [Milton] was the Covering Cherub & within him Satan" (II.37.8), and then enters into Milton.

---

[36] P & P, p. 841.

Blake next turns to Satan, who looms "a Twenty-seven-fold mighty Demon Gorgeous & beautiful" (II.38.11-12). Yet Satan too appears in the familiarizing setting:

> Loud Satan thunderd, loud & dark upon mild Felpham shore
> . . . he howld round upon the Sea.
>
> (II.38.13-14)

Blake stands "in Satans bosom & beheld its desolations" (II.38.15), and the elevated tone of the language he uses to describe what he sees shows that Blake is in the presence of the archetypal:

> A ruind Man: a ruind building of God not made with hands
> . . .
> Its furnaces of affliction in which his Angels & Emanations
> Labour with blackend visages among its stupendous ruins
> . . .
> In which dwells Mystery Babylon, here is her secret place
> . . .
> Here is her Cup filld with its poisons, in these horrid vales
> And here her scarlet Veil woven in pestilence & war
>
> (II.38.16-26)

Satan here is the Antichrist, and he provokes the Christlike speech from Milton which is gathering in force from plate 32 to the trumpet fanfare of plate 41. Milton's declaration of "Self Annihilation" only drives Satan to reveal his true nature once and for all (and presumably Blake is still standing "in Satans bosom") for Blake to reject, however it may appear in the future: Satan is the "collective psyche" commanding obedience. Satan's command here to Milton and Blake to "fall therefore down & worship me" may seem like a futile gesture at this point, but not completely when we remember his past behavior in the Bard's Song, all included in the symbol here as part of its background of significance. For there *had* been a time (and not so long ago) when all around him had "submit[ted] . . . to [his] eternal Will & to [his] dictate" (II.38.52-53).

Then, Blake and Milton had explored the Ulro that opened within Satan's bosom, searching out the collective unconscious in all its most fearsome aspects. Satan's speech *here* instead vitalizes the most powerful archetypes of the Self against the submission to the collective will that Satan demands.

At first the forms taken by this archetype are multiple; as plate 39 proceeds, there is an increasing unification of them into the one symbol. Around Milton (who is "on [Blake's] path") suddenly "the Starry Seven Burnd terrible" (II.39.3-4). No longer the Seven Eyes of God, the Seven have assumed "Forms Human" and now have "Starry limbs." The experience of the Regeneration of Self (in Jung's sense of the word "Self") with which the rest of these plates are occupied is focused upon Blake as the individual at Felpham, for these Seven "st[an]d in a mighty Column of Fire Surrounding Felphams Vale" (II.39.8-9). They call for Albion to awake, and "the Four Zoa's awake from Slumbers of Six Thousand Years" (II.39.13). Around Albion's still sleeping body Satan now circles, like Jung's "dark son of God":

> An awful Form eastward from midst of a bright Paved-work
> Of precious stones by Cherubim surrounded: so permitted
> (Lest he should fall apart in his Eternal Death) to imitate
> The Eternal Great Humanity Divine surrounded by
> His Cherubim & Seraphim in ever happy Eternity.
>
> (II.39.24-28)

Outside all of these concentric circles surrounding Albion are "Chaos: Sin on his right hand Death on his left And Ancient Night" (II.39.29-30).

Finally Albion does awake and arise, not at all the regenerated human Albion of Night Nine in *The Four Zoas*. Here he is the body politic, which is "seen by the visionary eye":

> . . . London & Bath & Legions & Edinburgh
> Are the four pillars of his Throne; his left foot near London
> Covers the shades of Tyburn: his instep from Windsor
> To Primrose Hill stretching to Highgate & Holloway . . .
>
> (II.39.35-38)

And on through all of the British Isles. His sight is at last aroused as well, for "He views Jerusalem & Babylon, his tears flow down" (II.39.48). At this sight of the terrors of contemporary society, his "strength failing . . . down with dreadful groans he sunk upon his Couch In moony Beulah" (II.39.50-52). There is only the mythic form of Blake to keep Albion from falling into another despairing sleep, for "Los his strong Guard walks round beneath the Moon" (II.39.52). Again Blake centers everything upon the mundane, limited present, for "Milton Labourd . . . here before My Cottage midst the Starry Seven, where the Virgin Ololon Stood trembling in the Porch: loud Satan thunder'd on the stormy Sea Circling Albions Cliffs" (II.39.56-60).

Ololon is not yet reunited with Milton, for she is still "the Virgin Ololon." Her subterranean anima tie with Leutha is recalled and then released. In the Bard's Song, Leutha had "stupified the masculine perceptions And kept only the feminine awake," and the result was a complete abandonment to the unconscious, which the masculine perception would not acknowledge. Ololon here sees that present-day philosophies that would totally structure intuitive knowledge have their origins in the male's refusal to recognize the unconscious:

> Are those who contemn Religion & seek to annihilate it
> Become in their Femin[in]e portions the causes & promoters
> Of these Religions, how is this thing? this Newtonian
>   Phantasm
> This Voltaire & Rousseau: this Hume & Gibbon &
>   Bolingbroke
>
> (II.40.9-12)

Self-accusing, Ololon seeks to hide her face and lets her tears fall; and Rahab appears in answer as Satan had to Milton's earlier speech of "Self Annihilation." As an archetype of the Self had risen up when Satan called for obedience, so Milton in plate 41 speaks "in terrible majesty" the ultimate wisdom of the poem that is to be passed on to Blake.

The message of this plate is that *one must let go*. One must "wash off the Not Human," "cast off Rational Demonstration," "cast off Bacon, Locke & Newton from Albions covering"—finally, cast off self-doubt. We can see how necessary Milton is for Blake when we consider that the "filthy garments" that Milton "takes off" are all of the most immediate charges that Blake has faced in his own mind from his "corporeal friends," Hayley, even his earlier teachers of art. "It no longer shall dare to mock with the aspersion of Madness Cast on the Inspired" (II.41.8-9). Blake had bitterly written in his Notebook, "To F——— [most probably Flaxman], I mock thee not tho I by thee am Mocked Thou callest me Madman but I call thee Blockhead." Nor shall Inspiration be ridiculed "by the tame high finisher of paltry Blots, Indefinite, or paltry Rhymes; or paltry Harmonies" (II.41.9-10). Blake had noted in his "Annotations to the Works of Sir Joshua Reynolds" of his master Moser when he was studying art: "I was once looking over the Prints from Rafael & Michael Angelo . . . Moser came to me & said You should not Study these old Hard Stiff & Dry Unfinishd Works of Art, Stay a little & I will shew you what you should Study. He then went & took down Le Bruns & Ruben's Galleries How I did secretly Rage. I also spoke my Mind."[37] Blake wrote of Hayley's efforts to promote portrait painting: "Portrait Painting is the direct contrary to Designing & Historical Painting in every respect."[38] Again, "Mr. H . . . is as much averse to my poetry as he is to a Chapter in the Bible. . . . Mr. H. approves of My Designs as little as he does of my Poems."[39] Those Deists mentioned by Ololon are also "cast off" as "the idiot Questioner who is always questioning, But never capable of answering; who sits with a sly grin . . . Who publishes doubt & calls it knowledge; whose Science is Despair . . ." (II.41.12-15).

This *letting go* has been the message of the whole poem as well, and Blake has learned to express his wrath as well as his pity. The suppression of anger and genius was let go in the

[37] *Ibid.*, p. 628.
[38] Keynes, ed., *Letters of William Blake*, p. 59.
[39] *Ibid.*, pp. 69-70.

Bard's Song, Jealousy was let go by the "Daughter of Beulah," both Milton and Ololon "Annihilate" their "Selfhoods." That splendid plate 32 which shows Blake falling back onto his garden path as the star enters his foot is of a man opening all guards, with his head flung back so that he faces, not the brilliant flames surrounding the star and the name "William," but the darkness that borders everything in the plate. In the very similar plate 37, labelled "Robert" (Blake's dear dead brother), the figure is quite enveloped by the darkness, which is lit up by the falling star of Milton.

At this, "the Virgin Ololon" finally unites with Milton, recognizing that they exist as Contraries to one another—that "marriage" of opposites again. In her sight, "the Void Outside of Existence . . . if enter'd into Becomes a Womb" (II.41.36—42.1). This is a phrase that Blake repeats over the archway in his drawing that begins *Jerusalem* (though later erased). This drawing shows Los entering the chaos in "Albions bosom" with his globe of fire, so we see how important is this change in Blake's perception of the principle of chaos: "if enter'd into" it produces, not extinguishes, life.

Ololon casts off her "virginity," and at last merges with Milton. Together they appear in "Felphams Vale," where Blake stands waiting by his cottage, and that is the last that we see of them. Neither is necessary for Blake any longer. Those archetypes of the Self that had appeared in plate 39 surround Blake again as "with one accord the Starry Eight bec[o]me One Man Jesus the Saviour" (II.42.10-11). As a result, Blake envisions the materials of his other two prophetic poems. "The Twenty-four Cities of Albion [which] arise upon their Thrones to Judge the Nations of the Earth" appear again at the conclusion of *Jerusalem* to weigh and find wanting "the Kingdoms of the World & all their glory that grew on Desolation" (*J* IV.98-51). "The Immortal Four in whom the Twenty-four appear Four-fold" are to be met in greater detail in *The Four Zoas*, where they too finally "Ar[i]se around Albions body." And Jesus here "wept & walked forth From Felphams Vale clothed in Clouds of blood" as he is to appear throughout *The Four Zoas* and *Jerusalem*. *This* is to be the apocalypse to come, to be celebrated in Blake's poetry evidently, for "then to their mouths the Four Applied their Four Trumpets & them sounded to the Four winds" (II.42.22-23).

Blake's reaction in that Vale is to be expected of the man who has encountered the archetype directly: terror and trembling as the energy that is not his passes to him. The concluding lines of *Milton* are all-significant: Blake is the Bard for the sake of other men. There is no personal glory, and the wisdom that he has learned spreads from that Vale. His mythic-poetic characters move outwards: Los and Enitharmon over "the Hills of Surrey" and on to London; Oothoon to the "Vales of Lambeth," where her call for sexual liberation had first been sung to the Daughters of Albion; and Los down into London, where with "terrific . . . anger" he "listens to the Cry of the Poor Man."

Blake returns to the present tense for the final five lines, the tense with which *Jerusalem* is to open. No longer is the "Poets Song" concerned with the psychological "journey of immortal Milton" (*M* I.2.1-2). Rather its main interest is the "Harvest & Vintage of the *Nations*" [italics added]. Both the myth ("Rintrah & Palamabron") and the historic materials ("All Animals upon the Earth") stand ready to be ordered by the mythmaker whose ego is now lost in theirs in the best and noblest sense.

FIVE

Beyond Myth, Beyond Non-Myth

BLAKE indeed sings "of the
Sleep of Ulro! and of the passage through Eternal Death!" in
Jerusalem, as the first lines of that poem promise. He renders
chaos in its "Minute Particulars," and that polarity does not
appear here as "the soul-shuddring vacuum," "Voidness," "the
Abyss," or "Eternal Death." Instead the characters endure the
horrors of modern warfare, industrialism, and the reactionary
political climate of early nineteenth-century England. It is as if
we are taken into the world of the chants of Ahania and Enion
in *The Four Zoas*, or the Ulro through which Milton and Olo-
lon pass in *Milton*, and remain there until the apocalypse be-
gins. *Jerusalem* is a direct continuation of those two other
poems, however, for Blake here knows from the very begin-
ning that Albion's social disintegration is psychological in ori-
gin. The horrors of life in contemporary England increase in
direct proportion to Albion's resistance to descent into the un-
conscious and his struggle to deny its existence in himself. Los
sees this from the start, unceasingly calling on Albion to ac-
cept the "forgiveness of Sin" that both Jerusalem and Los feel
toward Albion, and to acknowledge the darkness within him-
self. *That* acknowledgment ultimately proves to be both the
motivation for and the fruition of the apocalypse.

Several passages set forth the poetic task that Blake has set
himself in this poem, and all recall the man whose "bones
trembled" as he "fell outstretchd upon the path A moment"
and who then rose in determination. These passages vigorously
assert the social function of the poet: the necessity for him to
"listen . . . to the Cry of the Poor Man" (*M* II.42.34), and the
equal necessity for him to listen to his own psychological expe-
rience which, far from being "private," only leads to knowl-

edge of public experience. Blake implores Jesus at the very
start, in words strongly recalling *Milton*:

> To open the Eternal Worlds, to open the immortal Eyes
> Of Man inwards into the Worlds of Thought: into Eternity
> Ever expanding in the Bosom of God . . .
> Annihilate the Selfhood in me, be thou all my life!
>
> $\qquad\qquad\qquad\qquad\qquad\qquad$ (1.5.18-22)

Later, Blake again speaks directly:

> . . . I heard in Lambeths shades:
> In Felpham I heard and saw the Visions of Albion
> I write in South Molton Street, what I both see and hear
> In regions of Humanity, in Londons opening streets . . .
> Cities . . .
> Are Men, fathers of multitudes, and Rivers & Mountains
> Are also Men; every thing is Human, mighty! sublime!
>
> $\qquad\qquad\qquad\qquad\qquad\qquad$ (2.34.40-48)

The quality of chaos has changed subtly from that of *The
Four Zoas*. It is intimately known and described in detail, no
longer feared as the unknown that threatens to overcome all
who "wander round repelld on the margin of Non Entity" (*FZ*
3.46.12). *Milton* set the precedent, though only after a consid-
erable amount of introspection: why not descend *with* Albion
as he "turns down the valleys dark" (*J* 1.4.22)? Why begin
the tale of Albion's dissociation, as Blake did in *The Four Zoas*,
by grandiloquently marshalling "the Aged Mother," the "Four
Mighty Ones" whose "Natures . . . the Heavenly Father only
[knoweth]," and innumerable "Fairies of Albion" and
"Daughter[s] of Beulah" (*FZ* 1.3.1—4.3)? For that matter,
why begin by invoking those "Daughters of Beulah" at all (*M*
2.1-21), even though the Wise Old Man had called upon his
Muses in *Paradise Lost*? Why not boldly start with one's *own*
experience in which one has tried to come to terms with disor-
der?

So Blake begins *Jerusalem* in the first person, telling of his
attempts to write the poem ("Trembling I sit day and night,

my friends are astonish'd at me"—1.5.16). The two "Contraries" are present, even intertwined, for Blake in the opening lines of the poem, as they were not in *The Four Zoas* until quite a lot of time had passed. Blake writes that the theme of "the Sleep of Ulro and . . . the passage through Eternal Death" calls him, and also "the awaking to Eternal Life." These twin themes appear to him "in sleep night after night" (that time when the underworld of the unconscious is traditionally dominant), and he awakes "ev'ry morn . . . at sunrise" (that time of clear consciousness) to see "the Saviour over [him] Spreading his beams of love, & dictating the words of this mild song" (1.4.4-5). Does that "mild song" refer to the sixteen-line speech immediately following, or does it refer to the poem as a whole? I am inclined to think the latter—and Blake's designation of this horrific lament for the separated Albion and Jerusalem as a "mild song" seems quite in keeping with the Blakean irony so familiar by this time. At any rate, it is clear that in *Jerusalem* (unlike *The Four Zoas* or *Milton*) the unifying archetype of the Self is present for Blake the poet from the start, and remains present during the poet's entire "passage through Eternal Death."

Blake resolves to write in this poem "of the building of Golgonooza" *and* "of the terrors of Entuthon" (1.5.24). These "terrors" are not the abstract "Abyss" nor the "draught of Voidness" near the beginning of *The Four Zoas*, which threatened "to draw Existence in" (*FZ* 2.24.1), but rather are those "terrible sons & daughters of Albion" whose names are so close to those who acquainted Blake with his own taste of Entuthon at his trial for sedition:

> . . . Hand & Hyle & Coban . . . Kwantok, Peachey,
>   Brereton, Slayd & Hutton . . .
> Scofield! Kox, Kotope, and Bowen [who] revolve most
>   mightily . . .
> . . . to desolate Golgonooza
> $$(1.5.25-29)$$

Blake then passes at once to Los, whose trials with his Spectre over Los's "friendship" with Albion clearly reflect Blake's own questions about how a prophet was to function in reactionary England. Blake does not appear directly in the poem again until the end of Chapter Three (save for a few brief places that seem involuntary), and the weight of the poem passes to Los, Los who in this poem is more clearly Blake than ever before in his poetry, and who is the true hero of *Jerusalem*.

Chapter One opens with Los constructing Golgonooza as he has done so many times before, most recently in *FZ* 7.87-90 and *M* 1.24-29. In *The Four Zoas*, he built it as a refuge against the "Eternal Death" that threatened him and Enitharmon, "fabricat[ing] forms divine" and "with the strength of Art bending [the flames'] iron points" so that Golgonooza "remaind permanent a lovely form inspird divinely human" (*FZ* 7.90.22-37) until later in Night Eight, when it was a battlement against the forces of the Antichrist. In *Milton*, Rintrah and Palamabron meet Los and Blake "at the gate of Golgonooza," also fearing that the "Eternal Death" of Deism, warfare, and commerce is overtaking the earth; and Los furiously sets to work with his anvils, furnaces, hammers, and bellows. In Chapter One of *Jerusalem*, it is a defense against the "Chasmal, Abyssal, Incoherent . . . Mundane Shell: above; beneath: on all sides surrounding Golgonooza" (1.13.53-55). It is "a . . . form . . . divinely human" for it is:

> . . . a building of pity and compassion . . .
> The stones are pity . . .
> Enameld with love & kindness . . .
>
>   (1.12.29-31)

and on through the list of building materials that Blake compares to human affections. This Golgonooza exists *in potentia*, as did the Golgonooza of Night Seven of *The Four Zoas*, being "all clos'd up till the last day, when the graves shall yield their dead" (1.13.11). Los's mental attitude as he creates Golgonooza in Chapter One of *Jerusalem* is also the same as it was in Night Seven: he sees man's internal chaos and therefore the paramount importance of the forgiveness of sins—sins of others and sins of oneself. As he reminds his Spectre:

> Pity must join together those whom wrath has torn in
> sunder . . .
> O holy Generation [Image] of regeneration!
> O point of mutual forgiveness between Enemies!
> Birthplace of the Lamb of God incomprehensible!
>
> (1.7.62-67)

Significantly, this knowledge that Los had reached in *The Four Zoas* and *Milton* only after many false starts and much suffering is apparent to him from the beginning of *Jerusalem*.

Jerusalem continues the basic theme of dissociation from *The Four Zoas*. Los has escaped that state (and so has Blake), but Albion and Jerusalem face the unconscious, as did the Zoas, and with the same tragic results. Their reactions to it again illustrate the two neurotic kinds of behavior possible in such a confrontal: Albion tries to construct a rigid moral code against it, and Jerusalem succumbs to it.

For what is Albion's "Sin" in *Jerusalem* but the experiencing of his unconscious, the indulgence of his seething though repressed desire for Vala? His Emanation tells of this in limpid, unreproving language:

> Albion lov'd [Vala]! he rent thy Veil! he embrac'd thee! he
> lov'd thee!
> Astonish'd at his beauty & perfection, thou forgavest his
> furious love:
> I redounded from Albions bosom in my virgin loveliness.
> The Lamb of God reciev'd me in his arms he smil'd upon us.
>
> (1.20.36-39)

But Albion groans in reply:

> O Vala! O Jerusalem! . . .
> The disease of Shame covers me from head to feet: I have no
> hope
> Every boil upon my body is a separate & deadly Sin.
>
> (1.21.1-4)

He behaves very much as Urizen did in *The Four Zoas* when Ahania confronted her Zoa with the evidence of the uncontrollable emotions of the "Human Heart" (*FZ* 3.42.10-12). Urizen created the Mundane Shell and then Ulro, always "petrifying all the Human Imagination into rock & sand" (*FZ* 2.25.6). Albion in his turn creates the "Wastes of Moral Law" (1.24.24). His "remembrance of Sin" (2.50.30) is in reality the only true sin, for it too "petrif[ies] all the Human Imagination." It is the old effort by Urizen to impose "one command, one joy, one desire . . . one Law" (*BU* 11.38-40) all over again. No more than could Urizen, can Albion admit that *he* could be the cause of all the social misfortunes about him.

> Thus Albion sat, studious of others in his pale disease:
> Brooding on evil: but when Los opend the Furnaces before him:
> He saw that the accursed things were his own affections,
> And his own beloveds: then he turn'd sick! his soul died within him.
>
> (2.42.1-4)

He turns on Los in repudiation of what Los has shown him from his "Furnaces," but this only activates Los's visions of the depths to which English citizens have sunk. And a few plates later in Chapter Three, Albion falls under the "Plow of Nations" to the "Rock of Ages" (3.57.12-16). That "Rock of Ages" sounds very like the "slimy bed" that finally received Urizen in the frozen wastes of the "nether Abyss" (*FZ* 4.52.20). Albion is not seen very prominently again until plate 94 near the end of the poem, where he still "cold lays on his Rock: storms & snows beat[ing] round him" (4.94.1) just before the apocalypse, still much like Urizen in his appearance.

Jerusalem behaves as Albion *should*, as she sees and then enters into Ulro. But she lacks the saving virtue of consciousness of Self, which Los does possess, and which will allow him to face social chaos in Chapter Three. And so she falls like Albion onto her own "Rock" until finally near the beginning of Chap-

ter Four "naked Jerusalem lay . . . all her foundations levelld
with the dust" (4.78.21-22). Her appearance in the poem is
gradual. When she is first separated from Albion in plate 5 of
Chapter One, her fate is like that of Enion and Ahania in *The
Four Zoas*: she "wander[s] away into the Chaotic Void, lament-
ing" (1.5.63). But her experience is different from that of
those Emanations. Rather than merely wandering on the
"margin of Non-Entity" (*FZ* 3.46.12), there to see the con-
temporary confusion threatening to overwhelm man, Jeru-
salem goes *into* that chaos. In Chapter Two, Jesus declares of
Jerusalem that:

> London is a stone of her ruins; Oxford is the dust of her
> walls!
> Sussex & Kent are her scatterd garments: Ireland her holy
> place:
> And the murderd bodies of her little ones are Scotland and
> Wales.
>
> (2.43.19-21)

Throughout the poem, the trials of Jerusalem are those
known by the Londoners around Blake and, through exten-
sion, by Blake himself. She sits in the mills with the workers
in Chapter Three, and at this point she has no controlling con-
sciousness with which to comprehend what she knows. She is
like the falling Tharmas who "bellowd oer the ocean thund-
ring sobbing bursting" (*FZ* 3.45.9). Jerusalem, in her turn, is
as lost in the unconscious as are the workers:

> . . . [sitting] at the Mills, her hair unbound her feet naked
> Cut with the flints: her tears run down, her reason grows like
> The Wheel of Hand. incessant turning day & night without
> rest
> Insane she raves upon the winds hoarse, inarticulate.
>
> (3.60.41-44)

In contrast to Albion and Jerusalem, Los possesses from the
very beginning of the poem the wisdom only reached by the
conclusions of *The Four Zoas* and *Milton*: the certainty that one

should incorporate, rather than try to transcend, the seeming formlessness of the unconscious. His journey in the poem is deeper and deeper into Ulro and "Eternal Death." He plunges bravely into the "interiors of Albions Bosom . . . entering the caves Of despair & death" (2.45.3-5), armed only with "his globe of fire," so that he may

> . . . walk . . . among
> Albions rocks & precipices! caves of solitude & dark despair
> And [see] every Minute Particular of Albion degraded & murderd.
>
> (2.45.5-7)

As Blake's agent, Los searches out the "Particulars" of Albion's morality of "Chastity" (produced by Albion's sense of his own lack of chastity), which has affected all British life with such terrible results. ("I am drunk with unsatiated love I must rush again to War: for the Virgin has frownd & refusd"—3.68.62-63.) Los's cry—"Are not Religion & Politics the Same Thing?" (3.57.10)—is central to Blake's point throughout the poem. Los *watches* in this poem as he has not before in Blake's poetry, and what he sees are the "Minute Particulars" of the unconscious. And through that watching he also reunifies. The "Divine Vision" keeps reappearing throughout the poem as things worsen, and that word "Vision" may be taken in several ways. Certainly it is a mystical appearance of Christ; it is also the act of envisioning what is happening. That "Divine Vision" which "became . . . a globe of blood wandering distant" (3.66.41-43) is described as a "burning flame" (3.66.41), but could as well be an eye. Like that "Divine Vision," Los sees the seeming triumph of Vala and the sons and daughters of Albion, but always within the larger framework. As Los resolutely tells his Spectre near the beginning of Chapter One (who is not so much evil as ignorant—he says rather pathetically to Los, "How can I then behold And not tremble" in 1.10.58-59), forgiveness of sin rather than rejection of it is necessary. It is in the imaginative rejoining of "Enemies" by "Pity" that Christ is continually re-

born, and as Los enters "Albions bosom" Los becomes truly
Christlike.

From the beginning Los "beholds," constantly searching
out what is around him. After Los builds Golgonooza in Chap-
ter One:

> [He] beheld his Sons, and he beheld his Daughters . . .
> And . . . the mild Emanation Jerusalem eastward bending
> . . .
> And Hand & Hyle rooted into Jerusalem by a fibre . . .
> . . . a mighty Polypus growing
> From Albion over the whole Earth: such is my awful Vision.
> (1.14.16—15.5)

It is notable that Blake cannot help breaking into the first per-
son here, and, as Jesus bent over the "Human Polypus of
Death" in *The Four Zoas*, so Los-Blake observes the Polypus
here in all its minutiae, nor does he tremble as did his Spectre:

> I turn my eyes to the Schools & Universities of Europe
> And there behold the Loom of Locke . . .
> . . . many Wheels I view, wheel without wheel, with cogs
> tyrannic . . .
> . . . I see Albion sitting upon his Rock . . .
> And thence I see the Chaos of Satan . . .
> Hampstead Highgate Finchley Hendon Muswell hill . . .
> (1.15.14—16.1)

And on and on in what seems at first like wearying detail, but
soon becomes an "awful Vision" of the Ulro lying all around
Blake that involves the reader with its immediacy.

When Los told Enitharmon in *The Four Zoas* that "in the
Brain of Man we live, & in his circling Nerves" (*FZ* 1.11.15),
she scornfully replied that "Human Nature shall no more re-
main nor Human acts" (*FZ* 1.11.23), and proceeded to foretell
the results of the mythic war between Luvah and Urizen: "War
& Princedom & Victory & Blood" (*FZ* 1.11.24). Los's Spectre
describes chaos similarly in Chapter One of *Jerusalem*, when he
is trying to discourage Los's friendship for Albion, saying,

"Listen, I will tell thee what is done in moments to thee un-
known" (1.7.29), and then does so in terms of the myth:

> Luvah was cast into the Furnaces of affliction and sealed,
> And Vala fed in cruel delight, the Furnaces with fire . . .
>
> (1.7.30-31)

Yet Los's knowledge of chaos goes beyond this old story,
and he says, "I know far worse than this: I know that Albion
hath divided me" (1.7.51-52). And then come the passages in
which Los tells of the "terrible sons and daughters of Albion"
who persevere to "desolate Golgonooza," those outer correla-
tives of Blake's own interior struggles. In this second chapter,
what Los "beholds" is even "worse" than *that*: the warfare and
industrialism that come to seem predominant in Chapters
Three and Four. Significantly, he is receptive to what he sees,
not resisting it at all:

> Los was all astonishment & terror: he trembled sitting on
>   the Stone
> Of London: but the interiors of Albions fibres & nerves were
>   hidden
> From Los; astonishd he beheld only the petrified surfaces;
> And saw his Furnaces in ruins.
>
> (2.46.3-6)

Yet although Los does not turn away from this chaos, neither
does he succumb to it, for always he sees its "Minute Particu-
lars" and then goes on building. In Chapter One, he forced his
Spectre to

> Take thou this Hammer & in patience heave the
>   thundering Bellows
> Take thou these Tongs [and] strike thou alternate with
>   me . . .
>
> (1.8.39-40)

Here in Chapter Two, he sees "his Furnace in ruins," and also
the "Four Points of Albion reversd inwards," and immediately

He siezd his Hammer & Tongs, his iron Poker & his
  Bellows,
Upon the valleys of Middlesex, Shouting loud for aid
  Divine.

                                                    (2.46.8-9)

Similarly at an earlier point in Chapter Two, when Los and
"The Divine Family" watch Albion fall toward "Eternal
Death" (2.35-39), they all despair but Los, who "grew furious
raging" and proclaims what he sees:

. . . the blood of the English! we delight in their blood on
  our Altars!
. . . the Giants Hand & Scofield
Scofield & Kox are let loose upon my Saxons! . . .
I will not endure this thing! I alone withstand to death.

                                                    (2.38.48-71)

Chapter Three shows how one is to approach this disorder,
how to perform (as Blake calls it) "the Forgiveness of Sins."
There is something overwhelming about the effect of this
chapter. Blake presents nothing from contemporary life that
he has not already shown us, but previously he always did so in
passages or plates that were soon over and followed by evoca-
tions of Orc and his forces, Golgonooza, or the glories of the
apocalypse to come. Certainly, Night Eight of *The Four Zoas*
dwells upon the darkness of that night before the morning.
There "Urizen in self deceit his warlike preparations fabri-
cated" (*FZ* 8.101.26), the Females of Amalek sang their Song,
and the sons of Eden described the "mills" of Satan. But the
Contrary of the "Devourer" largely showed itself in the posses-
sion of Orc and Urizen by the archetype of the Antichrist, and
in the chants of Ahania and Enion, whose visions of "Universal
Death" were set in the framework of Blake's myth: Ahania saw
Albion decaying on his rock, and Enion saw the "Lamb of
God" coming to redeem mankind and Albion. While the ef-
fect was powerful, a distance was maintained between the
reader and that confusion. But in plate after plate of ac-

cumulating horror in Chapter Three of *Jerusalem*, Blake
searches the nature of what is all about him. The Song of the
Females of Amalek reappears almost word for word in *Jerusalem*
(3.67.44-62), but here it is part of the larger picture. The
modern warfare that Urizen "fabricate[s]" and the indus-
trialism of the Satanic "mills" are given to us in Chapter Three
of *Jerusalem* with every variation. It is as if Blake has finally let
the waters break, entering as never before into the depths of
life as it was being lived all around him.

Jesus best exemplifies the necessary "Forgiveness of Sins" in
his "Song" to Jerusalem who sits "at the mills," Jesus whom
Blake and Los both long to approximate since he (unlike them)
has gone beyond wrath to pity. This is not to say that wrath is
unnecessary, for it enables Los to keep on building Gol-
gonooza, chapter after chapter—and Blake to go through the
profound pain of "Entering into [those] Images" of the seem-
ing triumph of the Daughters of Albion and the Covering
Cherub of Chapters Three and Four. But that wrath changes as
the poem proceeds. "Pity must join together those whom
wrath has torn in sunder" (1.7.62), Los recognized near the
beginning of *Jerusalem*, and Blake uses that word "Pity" differ-
ently in this poem than he has before. No longer the "Pity"
that "make[s] somebody Poor" (*S. of E.*, "The Human Ab-
stract"), this "Pity" is the altogether different mental attitude
of "forgiveness."

While Los sits "terrified beholding Albions Spectre . . .
Spreading in bloody veins in torments over Europe & Asia"
(3.60.2-3), Jesus or the "Divine Vision" goes *into* those fur-
naces, "often walking from the Furnaces in clouds And flames
among the Druid Temples" (3.60.6-7). His Song to the de-
spairing Jerusalem there is "sung by slaves," further emphasiz-
ing his experience of the bondage which she knows. As he de-
clares to her, he too is "bound . . . down upon the Stems of
Vegetation" (3.60.11). He tells her what she already knows:
like Blake's fellow Englishmen, she is experiencing the horrors
of famine, war, and general disintegration. He promises her
reintegration by remaining with her in the chaos:

. . . I will lead thee thro the Wilderness . . .
And in my love I will lead thee

(3.60.36-37)

Her answering speech recognizes that Jesus' essential attitude is acceptance, rather than the terror that is the attitude of Los, since Jesus "knowest [she is] deluded by the turning mills" (3.60.63). Jesus' reaction to her situation is much the same as his reaction to the "Human Polypus of Death" in pages 55-56 of *The Four Zoas*, for he says to her:

. . . Pitiest thou these Visions of terror & woe!
Give forth thy pity & love, fear not! lo I am with thee
always

(3.60.66-67)

As with Enion's chant "from the Caverns of the Grave" in Night Eight of *The Four Zoas*, what is being urged (here by Christ and there by Enion) is the perception of the "Divine Vision" *while in* chaos.

Jesus elaborates upon "the Forgiveness of Sins," and we see that it is eternal process, an anticipation of the dynamic "going forward . . . irresistible from Eternity to Eternity" (4.98.27). Jesus tells Jerusalem that without the Sin there could be no forgiveness, without the descent there could be no ascent. Mary justifies her "impure" and decidedly earthly pregnancy to Joseph:

. . . if I were pure, never could I taste the sweets
Of the Forgiveness of Sins! if I were holy! I never could
behold the tears
Of love

(3.61.11-13)

Joseph's answer is couched in language that is close to the concluding plates of Chapter Four, suggesting that his is the final wisdom to be reached:

. . . Jehovahs Salvation
. . . [is] the Continual Forgiveness of Sins

In the Perpetual Mutual Sacrifice in Great Eternity! . . .
. . . And this is the Covenant
Of Jehovah: If you Forgive one-another, so shall Jehovah
  Forgive You.

                                              (3.61.21-25)

And in Chapter Four:

   . . . Forgiveness of Sins which is Self Annihilation. it is the
   Covenant of Jehovah.

                                              (4.98.23)

Jesus has promised Jerusalem to "lead [her] thro the Wil-
derness" (3.60.36), and so he does both metaphorically and
psychologically. As he tells her of Mary (so like herself) who
also had seemed lost in the desert wilderness:

   . . . The Chaldean took
   [Her] from [her] Cradle. The Amalekite stole [her] away
      upon his Camels
   Before [she] had ever beheld with love the Face of Jehovah.

                                              (3.61.40-42)

he also shows her that that "Wilderness" is an essential part of
the "Perpetual Mutual Sacrifice." For as Mary declares:

   . . . If I were Unpolluted I should never have
   Glorified thy Holiness, or rejoiced in thy great Salvation.

                                              (3.61.45-46)

Jesus is also reminding Jerusalem of her own potentially unifi-
able Self (in Jung's sense of the word "Self") as he tells her that
"Every Harlot was once a Virgin: every Criminal an Infant
Love!" (3.61.52). It is not a vision that she is able yet to com-
prehend fully, for she replies, "I am an outcast." Still, she *is*
able to say feebly: "I know that in my flesh I shall see God"
(3.62.16).

   This "Song" of Jesus is followed almost at once by nine ter-
rible plates of the "Sins" that must somehow be forgiven, and
it becomes obvious as the plates progress that this "forgive-
ness" of which Jesus speaks will not be glib or easy. Los's reac-

tion to them is not very different from Jerusalem's as he goes
into the horror that she too knew "closd in the Dungeons of
Babylon" (3.60.39). Significantly, just before Los "descends"
into these nine plates, he is given a vision of the preservation of
order in the midst of chaos:

> . . . Los beheld the Divine Vision *among* the flames of the
>   Furnaces
> Therefore he lived & breathed in hope (italics added).
>
> (3.62.35-36)

Yet still Los is driven to a state which is close to the dissocia-
tion of Jerusalem as he sees the modern warfare, the indus-
trialism keeping youth "in sorrowful drudgery," the triumph
of contemporary Druidism, and the dominance of Rahab,
Vala, and all of the sons and daughters of Albion. After Los
witnesses it all he "shout[s] with ceaseless shoutings & his
tears pour down His immortal cheeks" (3.71.56-57).

And indeed, at the end of Chapter Three there seems no res-
pite possible from "the Spectres of the Dead [who] howl round
the porches of Los . . . to devour the Body of Albion, hung-
ring & thirsting & ravning" (3.73.46-48). But at this point,
Blake again steps into the poem and asks the "Holy Spirit" to
"teach [him] . . . the Testimony of Jesus," words that recall
the opening of Chapter One in which "the Saviour over me . . .
dictat[ed] the words of this mild song" (1.4.4-5). This "Tes-
timony of Jesus" thus frames the first three chapters, which
form a complete unit in themselves that is a preparation for
what is to come in Chapter Four. Simultaneous with the de-
scents of Albion and Jerusalem into the unconscious has been
the development of Los's knowledge of that unconscious as he
has gained the necessary experience of it, which will serve as
the ground for his final Christlike vision in plates 90-93 of
Chapter Four. In this concluding "Testimony" (3.74.14—
75.22), Blake recapitulates the dissociations of Albion and
Jerusalem that have gone on in the previous chapters, and pre-
dicts the Chapter that is to come, when Christ and Antichrist
will be reabsorbed into each other as

> . . . Jesus breaking thro' the Central Zones of Death & Hell
> Opens Eternity in Time & Space; triumphant in Mercy.
>
> (3.75.21-22)

The closing lines of Chapter Three allude again to the eternal
process that Jesus said was the essence of "Jehovah's Cove-
nant": the "Continual Forgiveness of Sins" and the "Perpetual
Mutual Sacrifice." That process will be essential to the
apocalyptic conclusion of Chapter Four:

> . . . where Luther ends Adam begins again in Eternal Circle
> To awake the Prisoners of Death; to bring Albion again
> . . . into light eternal.
>
> (3.75.24-26)

The counterpoint of opposites is the informing structure of
the plates leading up to the apocalypse in Chapter Four (plates
78-93), although at first glance there may seem to be no form
at all to these "Last Days." Plates 78-84 contrast the percep-
tion of Jerusalem with that of Vala and the daughters of Al-
bion, those two aspects of the archetype of the Feminine. To-
gether, they describe the seeming domination of the world by
the Antichrist. They are answered by Los's vision of the unified
Jerusalem in plates 85-86, a vision very similar in purport to
the earlier "Song" of Jesus in which he promised to "Resur-
rect" Jerusalem (3.62.18-29). When the "Covering Cherub"
finally appears on plate 89 in his "majestic image of Selfhood,"
he causes Los in plates 90-93 to declare in "thunderous
Words" the Christlike wisdom he has learned in the course of
the previous chapters: Antichrist once again balanced by
Christ.

One can see Jerusalem's beginning reintegration in her fine
speech in plates 78-79, for she is no longer the "hoarse, inar-
ticulate" and "raving" creature of Chapter Three. Passionately
employing both the rhetoric and the metaphors of Hebrew
prophets, she is the Great Mother lamenting the fate of her
lost children. Her cherishing solicitude encompasses all of the
present-day world: France, Germany, "the swarthy sons of
Ethiopia"—on and on. They are all her "little-ones" (4.79.55)

who had once worshipped the "Lamb of God" with her, but now are "shrunk to a narrow doleful form . . . in narrow vales" (4.79.63-65). As she says, "I walk weeping in pangs of a Mothers torment for her Children" (4.80.2). She may conclude, "I am a worm, and no living soul!" (4.80.3), but the force of the preceding eighty-five lines certainly contradicts that. The comprehensiveness of her vision as she surveys the plight of her "little-ones" approaches that of Los, and her recollection of the days when her "children" "stood round the Lamb of God Enquiring for Jerusalem" (4.79.51-52) effectively preserves at least the possibility of that lost wholeness.

The howling "Lamentation" of Vala follows. She dominates the next two plates, together with Rahab and the Daughters of Albion, all "glowing with beauty & cruelty . . . [so that] no eye can look upon them" (3.66.33-34). All act like the uroboric "Devouring Mothers" that I discussed in Chapter Two. Their actions are undulating and serpentine:

> [Vala] . . . weav[ing] Jerusalem a body according to her will
> a Dragon form . . . The Serpent Temples thro the Earth
> . . . resound with cries of Victims
>
> (4.80.35-49)

> Rahab . . . refusd to take a definite form . . . stretchd out in
> length or spread in breadth
>
> (4.80.51-54)

> Cambel . . . drawing out [Hand] fibre by fibre
>
> (4.80.58-61)

Their effect upon their consorts is uroboric also, for as their "Female Wills" triumph their men become impotent, dependent children:

> Is the Cruel become an Infant
> Or is he still a cruel Warrior? look Sisters, look!
>
> (4.81.8-9)

> The mighty Hyle is become a weeping infant
>
> (4.82.8)

> Gwendolyn saw the Infant in her sisters arms . . .
> . . . and she also . . .
> . . . began her dolorous task . . .
> . . . to form the Worm into a form . . . by tears & pain
>
> (4.82.72-76)

A brief analysis of that "Female Will" from the viewpoint of Jungian psychology is in order here, since not a few critics (mostly feminist) have accused Blake of being a secret misogynist: one more chauvinist male who condemns feminine independence. The Jungian concept of the anima was discussed in Chapter Two, and the corresponding concept of the animus in the woman is pertinent here. The animus is the "man within" the woman, as the anima is the "woman within" the man; the animus is "the deposit . . . of all woman's ancestral experiences of man . . . a creative and procreative being . . . in the sense that he brings forth . . . the spermatic word."[1] Since it is an archetype, the animus has its negative side. When it is excessively present in a woman (or, as Jung would say, when she is "possessed by her animus"), it causes her to produce "infallible" opinions and dogmatic "laws," dominating those around her in an overbearing and self-righteous way: an exact description of Blake's "Female Will." The real terror and cruelty of the uroboric females in plates 81-82 are their *lack* of individual wills as they completely internalize society's laws of conservatism and repression, and then require all who love them to follow these laws without question. Jerusalem realizes this when she says:

> Tell me O Vala thy purposes . . .
> Wherefore in dreadful majesty & beauty outside appears
> Thy Masculine from thy Feminine hardening against the
>   heavens
> To devour the Human!
>
> (4.79.68-72)

So Vala proclaims throughout *Jerusalem* that according to

---

[1] C. G. Jung, *Two Essays*, p. 209.

the rigid Mosaic code Albion is vile for fornicating with her, and so is Jerusalem for forgiving him:

> My Father gave to me command to murder Albion . . .
> We soon revive them in the secret of our tabernacles
> But I Vala . . . keep his body embalmd in moral laws
>
> (4.80.16-27)

The Daughters of Albion in their climactic plates 65-71 in Chapter Three and plates 80-82 in Chapter Four likewise glory in those contemporary manifestations of an essentially patriarchal social structure: Druidism, expansionist warfare, industrialism, the "Religion of Chastity" (3.69.34), which holds that the woman has no innate sexual desire.

When Los answers Vala and these Daughters with his vision of Jerusalem in plate 86, "Jerusalem & Vala cease to mourn" (4.85.15). His vision echoes two sections from *Revelation*. Set in the context of Blake's poem, the first foretells the ultimate unity of the Zoas and the second that of Albion with Jesus. Jerusalem appears "Wingd with Six Wings . . . lovely Three-fold In Head & Heart & Reins" (4.86.1-3), causing Los to exclaim, "Holiness to the Lord" (4.86.4). Similarly, John saw the four Zoas that Ezekiel had seen at Chebar, "each of them six wings about him . . . saying, Holy, holy, holy, Lord God Almighty" (*Rev.* 4:8). Lines 14-21 are taken more or less directly from Chapters 21 and 22, where John envisions the New Jerusalem descending.

Yet though these sources may form the background of this passage, they give no hint of its life. John's vision of the New Jerusalem was of a city built of jasper, gold, and various precious and semiprecious stones—all fixed, even static, nonorganic substances without any hint of the human about them. Los's vision, however, pulses with life and movement, and though his Jerusalem is "coverd with immortal gems," those gems seem to take on a breathing life from her. Her forehead is a "Gate of Pearl Reflect[ing] Eternity," her wings are "featherd gold . . . thence featherd with soft crimson of the ruby bright as fire" (4.86.4-8). The wings themselves are "of gold

& silver," moving back and forth to cover and then reveal her "Reins."

Los's vision shows how Christlike Los is becoming. The circumstances of Jesus' earlier "Song" and this passage are similar. In Chapter Three, "the Divine Vision appeard . . . within the Furnaces . . . often walking from the Furnaces" (3.60.5-6), and his Song to Jerusalem was "sung by Slaves in evening time" (3.60.38). Here, Los "walks from Furnace to Furnace directing the Labourers . . . [and] sing[ing] on his Watch" (4.85.20-21). In his Song, Jesus had predicted Jerusalem's possible psychological unification through acceptance of the "Wilderness" that she was experiencing. Los also sees that promised unified Self while he himself "walks upon his ancient Mountains in the deadly darkness" (4.85.10), and after he has seen all of that "Wilderness" that one can possibly see. As mentioned earlier, Los watches throughout the poem and *unifies through seeing*.

Then back swings the balance from this vision of Jerusalem, which is, after all, one of her presence after the apocalypse is completed and time is finished. As the following two plates make clear, Los is still separated from Enitharmon as Jerusalem is from Albion, still caught with her in the old syndrome of "scorn & jealousy" (4.88.22). The "Covering Cherub," the "Antichrist accursed," then bursts forth with a primitive energy almost matching that of the Antichrist in Night Eight of *The Four Zoas*. As was Urizen, he is a "Human Dragon terrible And *bright*, stretchd over Europe & Asia *gorgeous*" (italics added) (4.89.11-12). Like the Zoas that Ezekiel saw, his wings are "filld with Eyes," but the wings are "black" rather than the fiery amber of those earlier Cherubim, and they spring with deadening accuracy from his "Scalpulae and Os Humeri" (4.89.29). His darkness is a source of energy, for some sort of light glows from his blackness: his wings are "black as night But translucent their blackness as the dazling of gems" (4.89.36-37), and they glow "with fire as the iron Heated in the Smiths forge, but cold the wind of their dread fury" (4.89.41-42).

Significantly, his appearance is in many ways the reversed mirror image of the "Form" of Jerusalem that Los has just seen—the "Form" and the "majestic image of Selfhood" thus sharing a subterranean intimacy. Like that "Form," the Antichrist is "coverd with precious stones" (4.89.11); his head, while "dark [and] deadly," also "incloses a reflexion Of Eden" (4.89.14-15); "his Bosom wide reflects . . . the Fish-pools of Heshbon Whose currents flow into the Dead Sea by Sodom & Gomorra" (4.89.24-27), as her bosom revealed the twelve Tribes of Israel; he too has "above his Head high arching Wings black . . . spring[ing] upon iron sinews" (4.89.28-29), "Two Wings spring[ing] from his ribs of brass . . . black as night" (4.89.36), and from his loins "eyeless Wings" (4.89.41).

As the sons of Eden cried, "Assume the dark Satanic body in the Virgins womb O Lamb divine" (FZ 8.104.13-14), so Los cries here, "Come Lord Jesus take on thee the Satanic Body of Holiness" (4.90.38). Like them also, he is answered by the sight of Satan's followers "seeking to Vegetate the Divine Vision . . . becom[ing] One Great Satan" with a hermaphroditic appearance (4.90.41-43). As Urizen (taking Satan's side) then waged war with "Engines of deceit" and "hooks & boring screws" (FZ 8.102.15-16), so the Daughters of Albion who are part of the "One Great Satan" "scream . . . beneath the Tongs & Hammer . . . in the burning Forge" (4.90.44-45).

In reaction, Los gives his own "Testimony of Jesus," declaring what he has learned from watching throughout the poem. It is the message of Jesus to Jerusalem infused with vigor, a complex attitude in which "Sins" are "forgiven" but not numbly accepted. Los's command to "Go to these Fiends of Righteousness Tell them to obey their Humanities, & not pretend Holiness" (4.91.4-5) is close to Jesus' exclamation, "Doth Jehovah Forgive . . . Pollution only on conditions of Purity . . . Such is the Forgiveness of the Gods, the Moral Virtues of the Heathen, whose tender Mercies are Cruelty" (3.61.17-21). Los's insight that "He who would see the Divinity must see him in his Children" (4.91.18) expresses the basic meaning of Jesus' story of Joseph and Mary. Los's attitude in this passage is that of the warrior getting ready for the "spiritual warfare" to come, for his own participation in what he earlier said are "the two Sources of Life in Eternity[,] Hunting and War" (2.38.31).

Los at last shares the perception of Jesus, no longer "howling" and "wailing" as he beholds chaos, but rather envisioning "Mutual Forgiveness forevermore" (4.92.18). He knows that the present "Waking Death" is not to be feared, and with his crowning insight that Satan and all his forces are the "Signal of the Morning" (4.93.26) he makes the beginning of the apocalypse possible. These forces of the Antichrist thus impel existence forward to the apocalypse as they did in Nights Eight and Nine of *The Four Zoas*, for the very extremity of their darkness suggests that the process is about to go onward. In the suspended pulsebeat between Los's paradoxical proclamation that night may be a "Signal of the Morning" and the beginning movement toward that "Morning," a vast universal energy is let loose, as if the tension of polarities will pull apart existence if not somehow balanced:

. . . storms & snows beat round [Albion on his rock] . . .
Howling winds cover him: roaring seas dash furious against
  him
. . . the for-ever restless sea-waves [foam] abroad . . .
. . . deep heaves the Ocean black thundering!
                                              (4.94.1-16)

With the words "Time was Finished!" we experience again the interplay of polarities known at the end of *The Four Zoas*. Britannia is the first to awake, immediately perceiving the Antichrist within her and acknowledging it:

. . . O God O God awake I have slain
In Dreams of Chastity & Moral Law I have Murdered Albion!
Ah! . . .
O all ye Nations of the Earth behold ye the Jealous Wife.
                                              (4.94.22-26)

With this admission Albion also awakens in a passage strongly reminiscent of Night Nine of *The Four Zoas*. There:

> Each morning like a New born Man [he] issu[ed] with
>   songs & Joy
> Calling the Plowman to his Labour & the Shepherd to his
>   rest . . .
> . . . Tharmas brought his flocks upon the hill & in the Vales
>   . . .
> Among the wooly flocks The hammer of Urthona sounds
> <div align="right">(<i>FZ</i> 9.138.28-35)</div>

In *Jerusalem*, Albion:

> Compel[s] Urizen to his Furrow; & Tharmas to his
>   Sheepfold;
> And Luvah to his Loom: Urthona he beheld mighty
>   labouring
> (4.95.16-18)

As Jesus began the psychological reunification of Jerusalem by telling her of the "Continual Forgiveness of Sins," so he enables Albion to bear the terrible knowledge of internal chaos by similar words. Jesus' story of Mary and Joseph predicted the final action of Albion here for like Joseph, who accepted the "Pollution" of Mary and then saw her flow "like a River of Many Streams . . . & g[i]ve forth her tears of joy Like many waters" (3.61.28-30), Albion accepts his own "Sins" and so throws "himself into the Furnaces of affliction . . . the Furnaces became Fountains of Living Waters flowing from the Humanity Divine" (4.96.35-37).

These final plates of *Jerusalem* fulfill the prophetic lyric at the beginning of *Milton*, which has served as inscription on the gates to those nether regions:

> Bring me my Bow of burning gold:
> Bring me my Arrows of desire:
> Bring me my Spear: O clouds unfold!
> Bring me my Chariot of fire!

I will not cease from Mental Fight
Nor shall my Sword sleep in my hand:
Till we have built Jerusalem,
In Englands green & pleasant Land.

The Zoas at the conclusion of *Jerusalem* take their bows and fire their "Arrows of Love" at the "Druid Spectre," and "Clouds roll round the horns Of the wide Bow." The "Chariots of the Almighty" appear to continue this "Mental Fight," for they contain those intellectual correlatives of the Contraries: "Bacon & Newton & Locke, & Milton & Shakspear & Chaucer." And then Blake proceeds to build Golgonooza, his own "Jerusalem," in 98.12-40. We are approaching the heart of the experience.

Blake had lovingly constructed this "great City" before, in plates 28 and 29 of *Milton*, although in Chapter One of *Jerusalem* this City is simply waiting and incomplete. One can tell this since, rather than opening into Eden, the side facing Eden "is walled up, till time of renovation" (1.12.52); also, the gates are "closd" and guarded by "Genii . . . Gnomes . . . Nymphs . . . and . . . Fairies" (1.13.26-29). But in *Milton*, the Sons of Los all "labour[ed] incessant" on it. Some made "Cabinets richly fabricate[d] of gold & ivory," and other Sons "buil[t] Moments & Minutes & Hours And Days & Months & Years & Ages & Periods." The Minutes had "azure Tent[s] with silken Veils," the Days and Nights had "Walls of brass & Gates of adamant," the Months "a silver paved Terrace builded high," the Years "invulnerable Barriers with high Towers," the Ages moats "with Bridges of silver & gold," the Ages a circle of "Flaming Fire." Space becomes "an immortal Tent built by the Sons of Los" that surrounds every man, who sees it around him in his "neighborhood" focused as by a concave lens.

But that Golgonooza remained passive and ornamental, built out of the same nonhuman materials as John's Jerusalem in *Revelation* 21. Although plate 29 of *Milton* is splendid, plate 28 is boring. By contrast, plate 98 of *Jerusalem* has a surging vigor, and these "Visions of God" are constantly expanding, incorporating, and pulsating with life. The dominant impulse behind these final three plates is the dynamic movement of all existence on every level. Golgonooza is completely human in conception, and everything else is burned away (or washed away). We exist in the world of the archetypal. Again and again, Blake squares the circle. Golgonooza, always before the round city, comprises:

> . . . every Man [who] stood Fourfold. each Four Faces had.
> One to the West
> One toward the East One to the South One to the North.
> the Horses Fourfold . . .
> South stood the Nerves of the Eye. East in Rivers of bliss the
> Nerves of the
> Expansive Nostrils West, flowd the Parent Sense the
> Tongue. North stood
> The labyrinthine Ear.
>
> (4.98.12-18)

And again:

> . . . These are the Four Rivers of Paradise
> And the Four Faces of Humanity fronting the Four Cardinal
> Points
> Of Heaven . . .
>
> (4.98.25-27)

"Dim Chaos brightend beneath, above, around!" (4.98.14), and thus it is part of the "beautiful Paradises" being described. The "Covering Cherub" had wings "filled with eyes" in a demonic parody of Ezekiel's Cherubim; "dim Chaos" here is also many-eyed (suggesting that even the unconscious is being made conscious as consciousness "sees" through the "dimness"). But Blake calls Chaos "eyed as the Peacock," a beautiful and not frightening simile, calling to mind as it does a shimmering and ever-moving iridescence.

Gradually the "Husk" of man "evaporat[es] revealing the lineaments of Man," and man's "Body of Death" is driven outwards "in an Eternal Death & Resurrection"—"Eternal

Death" part of the infinite process leading to "Unity," evidently. As Milton had finally realized, "Self Annihilation . . . is the Covenant of Jehovah," and this itself is "the Forgiveness of Sins" (4.98.23). This "Forgiveness" is an ongoing psychological process rather than any static situation. The Zoas' movement as they "go . . . forward irresistible from Eternity to Eternity" (4.98.27) suggests a similarly dynamic relationship among man's psychological "functions." Blake "creat[es] exemplars . . . Creating Space, Creating Time" (4.98.30-31) as he did in plates 28 and 29 of *Milton*, but here they are made from the materials "of Childhood, Manhood & Old Age" and "every Word & Every Character Was Human . . . such was the variation of Time & Space" (4.98.33-37). The Zoas "walk . . . To & fro in Eternity as One Man"—the Self really finally experiencing unity "according to fitness & order" (4.98.40). Everything has become part of the City: "Eternal Death" is part of "Resurrection," "dim Chaos" has "brightend," and "the . . . Non Ens of Death" too is "seen in regeneration" with its quality preserved, which it had in *The Four Zoas*, of being "all tremendous" and "unfathomable."

Blake's proscription no longer holds that "the great and golden rule of art, as well as of life, is That the more distinct, sharp and wirey the bounding lines, the more perfect the work of art . . . Leave out this line and . . . all is chaos again."[2] For "dim Chaos" proves essential to these final plates, and the "Non Ens of Death" is equally part of this apocalyptic culmination of the myth as it is:

> Seen . . . terrific or complacent varying
> According to the subject of discourse . . .
> . . . according to the Expansion or Contraction . . .
> . . . vary[ing] as the Organs of Perception vary.
>
> (4.98.34-38)

And these "Organs of Perception" do vary constantly as the "One Man" walks "to & fro in Eternity," both "seen and see-

[2] *P & P*, p. 540.

ing." These lines recall Albion's regenerated vision at the end
of *The Four Zoas* as:

> The Expanding Eyes of Man behold the depths of wondrous
>   worlds
> One Earth one sea beneath nor Erring Globes wander but
>   Stars.
>   (*FZ* 9.138.25-26)

Blake steps into the poem as he did in *Milton*, revealing that
what seem to be his own words here are really those of
"Jehovah speak[ing] Terrific from his Holy Place" (4.98.40-
41). More chariots fly before his "Organs of Perception" bear-
ing "the Words of the Mutual Covenant Divine" in the form of
earthly living creatures (the only way we may recognize them,
after all). Those creatures, "starry & flaming," include the
predictable "Lion, Tyger . . . Eagle" as well as those that have
borne less favorable connotations in Blake's earlier works, the
"Horse, Elephant . . . Dove, Fly, Worm." Last of all, and
most clearly part of things, comes "the wondrous Serpent
clothed in gems & rich array" (4.98.44) who had been the
enemy before the apocalypse. All of these creatures have
learned the wisdom known by the "One Man," which is "the
Forgiveness of Sins according to the Covenant of Jehovah"
(4.98.45). They "Humanize" and together make a most sig-
nificant "Cry," for that "Cry" suggests that Blake has at last
grown able to bear the sight of social error without "becom-
[ing] what he beholds." It is the "Cry" of a man who has
learned all there is to know about Chaos, both inside and out.
    The Zoas have not "Annihilate[d]" the principle of Satan
but only the "Druid Spectre." The *principle* still exists as a
Contrary. The "Cry" of the "Living Creatures" declares the in-
substantiality of what seems to rule the world . . . and,
paradoxically enough, the terrible reality which still requires
the constant "Mental Fight." The fact that the "Cry" is
couched in rhetorical questions tells us that the "Druid
Spectre" at once must pass away and has not yet. There are still
the "Human Sacrifices For Sin in War & in the Druid Tem-

ples," still the imperialistic "Kingdoms of the World," which
expand as their citizens know the "Desolation The Fruit of Al-
bions Poverty Tree when the Triple Headed Gog-Magog Giant
Of Albion Taxed the Nations into Desolation" (4.98.48-53).
This is a triumphant "Cry" to be sure—these events are all ul-
timately "Spectrous"—but it is the day-to-day reality since it
is voiced "from all the Earth from the Living Creatures of the
Earth." And if "dim Chaos," "the all wondrous Serpent," and
"the all tremendous unfathomable Non Ens of Death" are part
of this final "great City of Golgonooza," then so is the "Druid
Spectre," which can only be "Annihilate" when one *enters into
it* and comprehends the chaos in oneself that answers to it.

The five lines that are "the End of the Song of Jerusalem"
tell us that Blake has reached that center where everything be-
comes archetypally symbolic of man's "psychic drama." Every-
thing has been "Humanized," "even Tree Metal Earth &
Stone," for "all Human Forms [have been] identified." To be
human is to enter into the continual and continuous process:

. . . living, going forth & returning wearied
Into the Planetary lives of Years Months Days & Hours
                                                    (4.99.2-3)

This is all seen from Blake's position, at last reached, as he
"repos[es] And then Awak[es] into his Bosom"—the bosom of
Jesus. We should remember the opening lines of the whole
poem, which state that Blake awakes to "see the Saviour over
me Spreading his beams of love, & dictating the words of this
mild song" (1.4.5). So the whole poem must have been seen
from Christ's perspective, since it is all going to happen again
and again. "And I heard the Name of their Emnations they
are named Jerusalem," is the very last line. We know from
plate 26 that another name for her is "Liberty among the Sons
of Albion," so the "Mental Fight" to gain liberty from the
"Druid Spectre" must proceed unceasingly. Emanations are
still separate from the "Living Creatures," although reunifica-
tion has started since there are no longer any manifestations of
the archetype of the Feminine except for the glowingly posi-

tive Jerusalem. As the Emanation of "All Human Forms," Jerusalem will over and over experience the unconscious and integrate it into her final perception, always through her descents possessing that "Form" of "Holiness to the Lord" which Los saw in plate 86.

In the context of Blake's epic poems, these five lines of plate 99 gather together all of the chaos that had seemed to yawn beneath the feet of Zoas and Emanations. "The soul-shuddring vacuum," the "Voidness" and "Non-Entity," the "Eternal Death," and "the all tremendous and unfathomable Non Ens of Death," all are now seen by Blake to be part of "the life of Immortality." These lines' concluding position in the poem lets us know that Blake has "heard" (4.97.5 and 4.98.40) them to be the "Words of Jehovah" that make possible all of God's other "Visions . . . in Eternity." We have entered into the endless apocalypse with Blake, and the long descent that began with Albion's "fall into Division . . . His fall into the Generation of Decay & Death" (*FZ* 1.4.4-5) has proved that there is no linear direction to existence after all: the ending *is* the beginning, down *is* up. Myth is no longer necessary; the chaotic contents of the unconscious (though not the unconscious itself) have been "humanized" into consciousness. Blake has nothing more to add.[3]

This study of Blake has taught me more than a possible interpretation of his myth and poetry, for the critical process of analysis itself has also made conscious my assumptions about the nature of literature and of literary criticism, which had previously remained more or less unconscious. For it seems to me that the work of art follows the same psychological laws as does the human imagination from which it came. It too must reach a knowledge of the unconscious and incorporate it into consciousness. It is essential here to remember Jung's distinction between the personal and collective unconscious, for I am

---

[3] Blake finished *Jerusalem* around 1820; he wrote no other poetry (or at least none that has survived) before his death in 1827.

not saying that the work of art reveals the personal unconscious of its creator. I am writing rather of the irrational and chaotic collective unconscious of all human experience, which continues to exist as a source of great vitality for the work of art whether its creator was neurotic or healthy. Indeed, I think that the nature of the artist has no bearing upon the work of art, since its very creation sets it apart as an independent entity with its own continuing life. With the infinite variety of means that is also characteristic of the human psyche as it strives for individuation, the work of art has as its ultimate goal the same balance of polarities. Art gives form, the structure of consciousness, but somehow it must come to terms with the unconscious as must the human psyche. Archetypal symbols function in literature to incorporate the unconscious into that consciously created artifice.

Criticism must function as much on the unconscious and intuitive level as on the conscious and cerebral one, for the critic must determine whether the true energy in the artistic creation works with or against the conscious intent of the writer. Only then can the critic begin to decide the significance of the archetypal symbolism in the literary work and the ways in which the archetypes present act to bring about wholeness (or, alternately, the ways in which wholeness is *not* achieved).

It is important here to understand the general way in which the Jungian analyst studies the patterns of archetypal symbols that a person has experienced in dreams and fantasies, for the procedure is similar to that of the Jungian literary critic in many ways. As mentioned in the Preface, archetypes are active agents of the unconscious, and their bipolar nature suggests ways in which the problem of seemingly irreconcilable opposites may be solved, ways which are not possible through reliance on consciousness alone. According to rational consciousness, it seems an impossible contradiction to suppose that polarities may be balanced, even related. Archetypal symbols may appear to remind a person of split-off parts of his psyche that must somehow be admitted and incorporated into that psyche, or they may help to strengthen a person's shaky ego when it is in danger of dissociation. So the individual reveals himself primarily in his involuntary *selection* of particular elements of the collective psyche, and in the pattern of archetypal symbols which appear in his dreams and fantasies. A related question both for the analyst and the individual is how the individual's ego is to come to term with these archetypes, which have a disturbingly powerful vigor of their own. Can one rest content with the mere recognition of their presence? If so, one creates a "permanent state of dissociation, a split between the individual and the collective psyche." The two must be differentiated, and the energy associated with the archetypes "brought into play through man's conscious attitude towards the collective unconscious."[4]

This is a central problem for the literary critic, as well. Cataloguing the archetypes present in a literary work is not a "key" to the hidden meaning of that work. What matters is how they dynamically affect that work, changing it as other archetypes are called into play and revealing what needs to be strengthened in the work, what needs to be balanced. (It is perhaps too obvious to mention that immersion in the writer's corpus is necessary before one can even begin to reach some idea of what aspects of what archetypes are appearing in the specific works.) Paradoxically, I have become convinced that any literary criticism based upon Jungian psychology can only proceed inductively, and not through any deductive application of theory to the literary work being studied. One begins by asking questions:

What attitude toward the unconscious does the writer show? (A seeming lack of any attitude toward it at all is itself revealing.)

What patterns of archetypal symbols can one see? And do these patterns use the negative or the positive aspects of the archetypes?

Is there agreement or is there opposition between the writer's conscious intention in the work (its announced

[4] Jung, *Two Essays*, pp. 97-99.

"theme") and the unconscious pattern of archetypal symbols revealed?

And—most important of all—where does the true energy in the work seem to lie?

Only then can "the Spectator . . . Enter into these Images in his Imagination approaching them on the Fiery Chariot of his Contemplative Thought," only then "would he arise from his Grave [and] . . . meet the Lord in the Air & . . . be happy."[5]

[5] *P & P*, p. 550.

Bibliography

Abrams, Meyer. *English Romantic Poets: Modern Essays in Criticism.* New York: Oxford University Press, 1960.

————. *The Mirror and the Lamp; Romantic Theory and the Critical Tradition.* New York: Oxford University Press, 1953.

————. *Natural Supernaturalism: Tradition and Revolution in Romantic Literature.* New York: Norton, 1971.

Adams, Hazard. *Blake and Yeats: The Contrary Vision.* Ithaca: Cornell University Press, 1955.

————. *William Blake: A Reading of the Shorter Poems.* Seattle: University of Washington Press, 1963.

Altizer, Thomas, J. J. *The Descent into Hell; A Study of the Radical Reversal of the Christian Consciousness.* Philadelphia and New York: Lippincott, 1970.

————. *The Gospel of Christian Atheism.* London: Collins, 1967.

————. *The New Apocalypse: The Radical Christian Vision of William Blake.* East Lansing: Michigan State University Press, 1967.

Bentley, G. E., Jr. *Vala or The Four Zoas.* Oxford: Clarendon Press, 1963.

———— and Martin K. Nurmi. *A Blake Bibliography; Annotated Lists of Works, Studies, and Blakeana.* Minneapolis: University of Minnesota Press, 1964.

Berry, George. *Premillennialism and Old Testament Prediction; A Study in Interpretation.* Chicago: University of Chicago Press, 1929.

Bishop, Morchard. *Blake's Hayley: The Life, Works, and Friendships of William Hayley,* 1951; reprint Freeport, N.Y.: Books for Libraries Press, 1972.

Blake, William. *Poetry and Prose of William Blake.* Edited by David V. Erdman with commentary by Harold Bloom. Second edition, Garden City, N.Y.: Doubleday, 1970.

Bloom, Harold. *Blake's Apocalypse; A Study in Poetic Argument.* Garden City, N.Y.: Doubleday, 1963.

————, ed. *Romanticism and Consciousness; Essays in Criticism.* New York: Norton, 1970.

————. *The Visionary Company; A Reading of English Romantic Poetry.* Garden City, N.Y.: Doubleday, 1961.

Bloom, Harold and Frederick Hilles, eds. *From Sensibility to Romanticism: Essays Presented to Frederick Pottle.* New York: Oxford University Press, 1965.

Bodkin, Maud. *Archetypal Patterns in Poetry; Psychological Studies of Imagination.* Oxford: Oxford University Press, 1934.

Boettner, Loraine. *The Millennium.* Philadelphia: Presbyterian and Reformed Publishing Company, 1957.

Brinton, Clarence Crane. *The Political Ideas of the English Romanticists.* London: Oxford University Press, 1926.

Bronowski, Jacob. *William Blake and the Age of Revolution.* New York: Harper and Row, 1965.

————. *William Blake, 1757-1827; A Man without a Mask.* London: Secker and Warburg, 1944.

Burch, Vacher. *Anthropology and the Apocalypse.* London: Macmillan, 1939.

Buttrick, George Arthur, and others, eds. *The Interpreter's Dictionary of the Bible.* 4 volumes. New York: Abingdon Press, 1962.

Caird, G. B. *A Commentary on the Revelation of St. John the Divine.* London: Adam and Charles Black, 1966.

Campbell, Joseph. *The Hero with a Thousand Faces.* Princeton: Princeton University Press, 1963 (Bollingen Series XVII).

————. *The Masks of God.* Vol. 1, *Primitive Mythology,* New York: Viking, 1959. Vol. 2, *Oriental Mythology,* 1962. Vol. 3, *Occidental Mythology,* 1964.

Cassirer, Ernst. *The Philosophy of Symbolic Forms.* Vol. 2, *Mythical Thought.* Translated by Ralph Manheim. 1925; reprint New Haven: Yale University Press, 1955.

Cirlot, J. E. *A Dictionary of Symbols.* Translated by Jack Sage. London: Routledge and Kegan Paul, 1962.

Clarke, Colin. *River of Dissolution: D. H. Lawrence and English Romanticism.* New York: Barnes and Noble, 1969.

Cobban, Alfred. *Edmund Burke and the Revolt against the Eighteenth Century; A Study of the Political and Social Thinking of Burke, Wordsworth, Coleridge, and Southey.* London: G. Allen and Unwin, 1929.

Cohn, Norman. *The Pursuit of the Millennium; Revolutionary Millenarians and Mystical Anarchists of the Middle Ages.* New York: Oxford University Press, 1970.

Couchard, Paul L. *The Book of Revelation: A Key to Christian Origins.* London: Watts and Co., 1932.

Cross, Frank, ed. *The Jung Codex, a Newly Recovered Gnostic Papyrus: Three Studies.* New York: Morehouse-Gorham, 1955.

Curran, Stuart and Joseph Wittreich, Jr., eds. *Blake's Sublime Allegory; Essays on "The Four Zoas," "Milton," and "Jerusalem."* Madison: University of Wisconsin Press, 1973.

Daiches, David. *A Critical History of English Literature.* Vol. 4, *The Romantics to the Present Day.* London: Secker and Warburg, 1969.

Damon, S. Foster. *A Blake Dictionary: The Ideas and Symbols of William Blake.* Providence: Brown University Press, 1965.

————. *William Blake, His Philosophy and Symbols.* New York: Houghton-Mifflin, 1924.

De Groot, H. B. "The Ouroboros and the Romantic Poets: A Renaissance Emblem in Blake, Coleridge and Shelley," *English Studies* 50 (1969), 553-564.

De Sola Pinto, Vivian, ed. *The Divine Vision; Studies in the Poetry and Art of William Blake.* London: V. Gollancz, 1957.

Dike, Donald A. "The Difficult Innocence: Blake's Songs and Pastoral," *English Literary History* 28 (1961), 353-375.

Dorfman, Deborah. *Blake in the Nineteenth Century: His Reputation as a Poet from Gilchrist to Yeats.* New Haven: Yale University Press, 1969.

Eliade, Mircea. *Cosmos and History; The Myth of the Eternal Return.* Translated by Willard Trask. New York: Bollingen Foundation, 1954 (Bollingen Series XLVI).

————. *Myth and Reality.* Translated by Willard Trask. New York: Harper and Row, 1963.

————. *Myths, Dreams, and Mysteries: The Encounter between Contemporary Faiths and Archaic Realities.* Translated by Philip Mairet. New York: Harper and Row, 1960.

————. *Patterns in Comparative Religion.* Translated by Rosemary Sheed, New York: Sheed & Ward, 1958.

————. *The Sacred and the Profane: The Nature of Religion.* Translated by Willard Trask, New York: Harcourt, Brace, 1959.

Empson, William. *English Pastoral Poetry.* New York: Norton, 1938.

————. *Some Versions of Pastoral.* London: Chatto and Windus, 1935.

The Book of Enoch. Translated by Richard Laurence. Glasgow: John Thompson, 1882.

Erdman, David V. *Blake, Prophet against Empire; A Poet's Interpretation of the History of His Own Times.* Princeton: Princeton University Press, 1954.

————, "The Symmetries of *The Song of Los,*" *Studies in Romanticism,* 16 (1977), 179-188.

————, annotator. *The Illuminated Blake.* Garden City, N.Y.: Doubleday, 1974.

———— and John E. Grant. *Blake's Visionary Forms Dramatic.* Princeton: Princeton University Press, 1970.

The Apocalypse of Ezra. Translated by G. H. Box. London: Society for Promoting Christian Knowledge, 1917.

Farrer, Austin. *A Rebirth of Images; The Making of St. John's Apocalypse.* Westminster: Dacre Press, 1949.

Fisher, Peter. *The Valley of Vision, Blake as Prophet and Revolutionary.* Toronto: University of Toronto Press, 1961.

Fordham, Michael. *The Objective Psyche.* London: Routledge and Kegan Paul, 1958.

Freud, Sigmund. *The Basic Writings of Sigmund Freud.* Translated by A. A. Brill. New York: Modern Library, 1938.

Frye, Northrop. *Anatomy of Criticism; Four Essays.* Princeton: Princeton University Press, 1957.

————, ed. *Blake: A Collection of Critical Essays.* Englewood Cliffs, N.J.: Prentice-Hall, 1966.

————. "Blake's Treatment of the Archetype," *English Institute Essays (1950).* New York: Columbia University Press, 1950.

————. *Fables of Identity: Studies in Poetic Mythology.* New York: Harcourt, Brace, 1963.

————. *Fearful Symmetry; A Study of William Blake.* Princeton: Princeton University Press, 1947.

————, ed. *Romanticism Reconsidered; Selected Papers from the English Institute.* New York: Columbia University Press, 1963.

Funk, Robert W., ed. *Apocalypticism.* New York: Herder and Herder, 1969.

Geertz, Clifford. "Religion as a Cultural System," in Michael Benton, ed., *Anthropological Approaches to the Study of Religion.* New York: Praeger, 1966.

Gennep, Arnold Van. *The Rites of Passage.* Translated by Monika B. Vizedom and Gabrielle L. Caffee. Chicago: University of Chicago Press, 1960.

Giametti, A. Bartlett. *The Earthly Paradise and the Renaissance Epic.* Princeton: Princeton University Press, 1966.

Gilchrist, Alexander. *Life of William Blake, "Pictor Ignotus," With Selections from His Poems and Other Writings.* 1863; reprint New York: Phaeton Press, 1969.

Gill, Frederick. *The Romantic Movement and Methodism; A Study of English Romanticism and the Evangelical Revival.* New York: Haskell House, 1966.

Gleckner, Robert F. *The Piper and the Bard; A Study of William Blake.* Detroit: Wayne State University Press, 1959.

Grant, John E. *Discussions of William Blake.* Boston: Heath, 1961.

Gray, John. *Near Eastern Mythology.* London: Hamlyn Publishing, 1969.

Guirand, Felix, ed. *New Larousse Encyclopedia of Mythology.* Translated by Patricia Beardsworth. Second edition, New York: Hamlyn Publishing, 1968.

Hagstrum, Jean H. *William Blake, Poet and Painter: An Introduction to the Illuminated Verse.* Chicago: University of Chicago Press, 1964.

Harper, George Mills. "Apocalyptic Vision and Pastoral Dream in Blake's *The Four Zoas,*" *South Atlantic Quarterly* 64 (1965) 110-124.

Helms, Randel. "Blake at Felpham: A Study in the Psychology of Vision," *Literature and Psychology* 22 (1971), 57-66.

———. "Orc: The Id in Blake and Tolkien," *Literature and Psychology* 20:1 (1969), 31-35.

Henderson, Joseph and Maud Oakes. *The Wisdom of the Serpent: The Myths of Death, Rebirth and Resurrection.* New York: George Braziller, 1963.

Hirsch, Eric D. *Innocence and Experience: An Introduction to Blake.* New Haven: Yale University Press, 1964.

Hirst, Désirée. *Hidden Riches; Traditional Symbolism from the Renaissance to Blake.* London: Eyre and Spottiswoode, 1964.

Hodgart, Patricia and Theodore Redpath, eds. *Romantic Perspectives: The Work of Crabbe, Blake, Wordsworth, and Coleridge, as Seen by Their Contemporaries and by Themselves.* London: G. G. Harrap, 1964.

Holland, Norman. *The Dynamics of Literary Response.* New York: Oxford University Press, 1968.

Hostie, Raymond. *Religion and the Psychology of Jung.* Translated by G. R. Lamb. New York: Sheed and Ward, 1966.

Jacobi, Jolande. *Complex, Archetype, Symbol in the Psychology of C. G. Jung.* Translated by Ralph Manheim. New York: Pantheon, 1959.

Jacobi, Jolande. *The Way of Individuation*. Translated by R.F.C. Hull. New York: Harcourt, Brace, and World. 1967.

Jonas, Hans. *The Gnostic Religion: The Message of the Alien God and the Beginnings of Christianity*. Boston: Beacon, 1963.

Jung, C. G. *Analytical Psychology: Its Theory and Practice. The Tavistock Lectures*. New York: Pantheon, 1968.

————. *Collected Works*. Edited by Herbert Read, Michael Fordham, Gerhard Adler, and William McGuire; translated by R.F.C. Hull. New York: Pantheon, 1953-1967; Princeton: Princeton University Press, 1967-1978 (Bollingen Series XX).

Volume 5. *Symbols of Transformation*. 1956; second edition, 1967.

Volume 6. *Psychological Types*. 1971.

Volume 7. *Two Essays on Analytical Psychology*. 1953; second edition, 1966.

Volume 8. *The Structure and Dynamics of the Psyche*. 1960; second edition, 1969.

Volume 9, part 1. *Archetypes and the Collective Unconscious*. 1959; second edition, 1968.

Volume 9, part 2. *Aion: Researches into the Phenomenology of the Self*. 1959; second edition, 1968.

Volume 11. *Psychology and Religion: West and East*. 1958; second edition, 1969.

Volume 12. *Psychology and Alchemy*. 1953; second edition, 1968.

Volume 13. *Alchemical Studies*. 1967.

Volume 17. *The Development of Personality*. 1954.

————. *Memories, Dreams, Reflections*. Translated by Richard and Clara Winston. New York: Pantheon, 1961.

————, and Carl Kerényi. *Essays on a Science of Mythology: The Myths of the Divine Child and the Mysteries of Eleusis*. Translated by R.F.C. Hull. Second edition, Princeton: Princeton University Press, 1963 (Bollingen Series XXII).

Kermode, Frank, ed. *English Pastoral Poetry, from the Beginnings to Marvell*. New York: Barnes and Noble, 1952.

Keynes, Geoffrey. *Blake Studies: Essays on His Life and Work in Seventeen Chapters*. London: R. Hart-Davis, 1949.

————, ed. *The Letters of William Blake*. London: Hart-Davis, 1968.

————. *A Study of the Illuminated Books of William Blake, Poet, Printer, Prophet*. New York: Orion Press, 1964.

Kirk, G. S. *Myth: Its Meaning and Functions in Ancient and Other Cultures*. Oxford, Berkeley, and Los Angeles: Oxford University Press and University of California Press, 1970.

Kluckhohn, Clyde. "Myths and Rituals: A General Theory," *Harvard Theological Review,* 35 (January 1942), 268-279.

Kroeber, Karl. *Romantic Narrative Art.* Madison: University of Wisconsin Press, 1960.

Langbaum, Robert. *The Poetry of Experience; The Dramatic Monologue in Modern Literary Tradition.* New York: Random House, 1957.

Langer, Susanne. *Feeling and Form.* New York: Scribner, 1953.

————. *Philosophy in a New Key.* Cambridge: Harvard University Press, 1942.

Lerner, Laurence. *The Uses of Nostalgia: Studies in Pastoral Poetry.* London: Chatto and Windus, 1972.

Lincoln, Eleanor, ed. *Pastoral and Romance; Modern Essays in Criticism.* Englewood Cliffs, N.J.: Prentice-Hall, 1969.

Loew, Cornelius. *Myth, Sacred History, and Philosophy; The Pre-Christian Religious Heritage of the West.* New York: Harcourt, Brace, 1967.

Long, Charles. *Alpha: The Myths of Creation.* New York: Collier 1963.

Margoliouth, Herschel. *Blake's "Vala."* Oxford: Clarendon Press, 1956.

————. *William Blake.* London and New York: Oxford University Press, 1951.

Mattoon, Mary Ann. Unpublished lectures for "The Psychology of C. G. Jung." University of Minnesota, 1973.

Monk, Samuel. *The Sublime: A Study of Critical Theories in Eighteenth-Century England.* New York: Modern Language Association of America, 1935.

Neumann, Erich. *Amor and Psyche: The Psychic Development of the Feminine.* Translated by Ralph Manheim. Princeton: Princeton University Press, 1956 (Bollingen Series LIV).

————. *Art and the Creative Unconscious; Four Essays.* Translated by Ralph Manheim. Princeton: Princeton University Press, 1959 (Bollingen Series LXI).

————. *Depth Psychology and a New Ethic.* Translated by Eugene Rolfe. New York: Putnam, 1969.

————. *The Great Mother; An Analysis of the Archetype.* Translated by Ralph Manheim. 1955; second edition Princeton: Princeton University Press, 1964 (Bollingen Series XLVII).

————. *The Origins and History of Consciousness.* Translated by R.F.C. Hull. New York: Pantheon, 1954 (Bollingen Series XLII).

Nurmi, Martin K. "Blake's Doctrine of Contraries; A Study in Visionary Metaphysics." Ph.D. dissertation, University of Minnesota, 1954.

———. Blake's "Marriage of Heaven and Hell": A Critical Study. Kent, Ohio: Kent State Press, 1957.

Paley, Morton D. Energy and the Imagination: A Study of the Development of Blake's Thought. Oxford: Clarendon Press, 1970.

———, ed. Twentieth-Century Interpretations of "Songs of Innocence and Experience": A Collection of Critical Essays. Englewood Cliffs, N.J.: Prentice-Hall, 1969.

Peckham, Morse. Beyond the Tragic Vision; The Quest for Identity in the Nineteenth Century. New York: George Braziller, 1962.

———. The Triumph of Romanticism: Collected Essays. Columbia: University of South Carolina Press, 1970.

Perry, John. Lord of the Four Quarters; Myths of the Royal Father. New York: G. Braziller, 1966.

Philipson, Morris. Outline of a Jungian Aesthetics. Evanston, Ill.: Northwestern University Press, 1963.

Philp, Howard. Jung and the Problem of Evil. London: Rockcliff, 1958.

Ploger, Otto. Theocracy and Eschatology. Translated by S. Rudman. Richmond, Va.: John Knox Press, 1968.

Poggioli, Renato. "The Oaten Flute," Harvard Library Bulletin 11 (1957), 147-184.

———. "The Pastoral of Self," Daedalus 88 (1959), 686-699.

Praz, Mario. The Romantic Agony. Translated by Angus Davidson. London and New York: Oxford University Press, 1933.

Raine, Kathleen. Blake and Tradition. 2 volumes. Princeton: Princeton University Press, 1968 (Bollingen Series XXXV).

Robinson, Henry Crabb. Blake, Coleridge, Wordsworth, Lamb, etc. Being Selections from the Remains of Henry Crabb Robinson. Edited by Edith J. Morley. Manchester: Manchester University Press, 1922.

Rosenfeld, Alvin H., ed. William Blake; Essays for S. Foster Damon. Providence, R.I.: Brown University Press, 1969.

Russell, D. S. Between the Testaments. Philadelphia: Fortress Press, 1960.

Schorer, Mark. William Blake; The Politics of Vision. New York: Vintage Books, 1959.

Singer, June K. The Unholy Bible; A Psychological Interpretation of William Blake. New York: Putnam, 1970.

Thompson, E. P. *The Making of the English Working Class.* New York: Pantheon, 1963.

Toliver, Harold E. *Pastoral Forms and Attitudes.* Berkeley and Los Angeles: University of California Press, 1971.

Underhill, Evelyn. *Mysticism; A Study in the Nature and Development of Man's Spiritual Consciousness.* New York: E. P. Dutton, 1911.

Vogler, Thomas A. *Preludes to Vision; The Epic Venture in Blake, Wordsworth, Keats, and Hart Crane.* Berkeley and Los Angeles: University of California Press, 1971.

Warner, W. J. *The Wesleyan Movement in the Industrial Revolution.* London and New York: Longmans, Green, 1930.

Wasserman, Earl R. "The English Romantics: The Grounds of Knowledge," *Studies in Romanticism* 4 (1964) 17-34.

————. *The Subtler Language: Critical Readings of Neoclassic and Romantic Poems.* Baltimore: Johns Hopkins Press, 1959.

Watts, Alan. *The Two Hands of God; Myths of Polarity.* New York: George Braziller, 1963.

White, Helen C. *The Mysticism of William Blake.* Madison: University of Wisconsin Press, 1927.

White, Victor. *God and the Unconscious.* Chicago: H. Regnery, 1953.

Wilkie, Brian. *Romantic Poets and Epic Tradition.* Madison: University of Wisconsin Press, 1965.

Willey, Basil. *The Eighteenth-Century Background; Studies on the Idea of Nature in the Thought of the Period.* New York: Columbia University Press, 1940.

Wilson, Mona. *The Life of William Blake.* Edited by Geoffrey Keynes, third edition, London and New York: Oxford University Press, 1971.

Wittreich, Joseph A., Jr. "The 'Satanism' of Blake and Shelley Reconsidered," *Studies in Philology* 65 (1968), 816-833.

Wingfield Digby, George. *Symbol and Image in William Blake.* Oxford: Clarendon Press, 1957.

Witcutt, W. P. *Blake: A Psychological Study.* Port Washington, N.Y.: Kennikat Press, 1946.

Woodring, Carl. *Politics in English Romantic Poetry.* Cambridge: Harvard University Press, 1970.

Index

Ahania: in *BA*, 20-22; in *FZ*, 62-63, 90-91
Albion: in *FZ*, 65-66, 92-95, 114-15; in *J*, 159-60, 177
America: A Prophecy, 26-30
Antichrist, *see* archetype
apocalypse: in *A*, 29-31; in *FZ*, 80-115; in *J*, 176-83; in *MHH*, 38-39; in *SL*, 35-36; Judeo-Christian, 37-38 and Chapters Two, Three; Jung on, 31-32
archetype: anima, 53-55; animus, 172-73; Antichrist, in *FZ*, 80-91, 96-97, 103, in *M*, 149-50, in *J*, 174-76; Christ, in *FZ*, 57-58, 65-66, 75-76, 92-94, in *J*, 157, 162-63, 166-68, 174; divine incest, 27; feminine, in *FZ*, 54-71, in *M*, 142-47; function of, 5-8, 51; function of, in literature, 184-86; Great Mother, in *FZ*, 54, 59-61, in *J*, 170-73; mandala, in *FZ*, 55-58, 65-66, 76-80, 84, 103-107; self in *M*, 150-54; Wise Old Man, 133-35 and ff

Beulah, 143-45
Blake, William: as mythmaker, 12-19, 25-27, 34-47, 123-24; at Felpham, 49-50, 119-21; identification with Urizen, 11-12, 16-19; on "true art," 10-11; persona, 120-21, 125-27; personal unconscious, 117-34; Shadow, 127-34. *See also* Milton as Wise Old Man archetype
Book of Ahania, 19-22
Book of Los, 22-25
Book of Urizen, 13-19

chaos, in *BA*, 20-22; in *BL*, 22-24; in *BU*, 14-19; in *FZ*, 50-115; in *M*, 129-30, 135; in *J*, 156-58, 160-83. *See also prima materia*; unconscious
Christ, *see* archetype
contraries, 43-47; in *FZ*, 114-15; in *J*, 181-83
Council of God, 57

Eliade, Mircea, 95-115
emanations: as archetype, 53-54. *See also* Ahania; Enion; Enitharmon; Jerusalem; Ololon; Vala
Enion, 54, 91-94, 104-107
Enitharmon, 54-55, 62, 75-79; Shadow of, 70-71
Europe: A Prophecy, 31-35

Female Will, 172-73

Golgonooza: in *FZ*, 73-79; in *M*, 140-42; in *J*, 158-59, 178-82
Great Mother, *see* archetype

Hayley, William, 119-21, 124-34

Individuation, 6-7. *See also* archetype; Jung; unconscious

Jerusalem, 160-61, 166-71, 182-83
Jung, C. G., as Romantic, 7-8; on apocalypse, 31-32; on archetypes: animus, 172; Antichrist, 81; Christ, 75; mandala, 56-57; Wise Old Man, 118-19; on individuation, 117-19; on marriage, 143-44; on persona, 117-18; on psychological

Jung, C. G. (*cont.*)
types, 126-27; on Shadow,
118; on unconscious, 5-8,
51-52, 133-34

Los, in *BL*, 22-25; in *BU*, 17-19; in
FZ, 66-67, 72-80; in *M*, 124-25,
128-29, 139-42; in *J*, 158 ff
Luvah, 58-61, 109-12

mandala, *see* archetype
Mental Traveller, 102
Milton, 116-54; "Bard's Song" in,
121-35
Milton as Wise Old Man archetype,
134-53

Ololon, 142-53
Orc, in *A*, 27-30; in *FZ*, 67-70,
84-85

pastoral, 103-107
prima materia: in *BU*, 14-19; in early
poems, 9; in *FZ*, 59-60. *See also*
chaos; unconscious

Satan: in *M*, 122-32, 149-50. *See
also* archetype, Antichrist

Song of Los, 25-26, 35-36

Tharmas, 64-65, 104-106
The Tyger, 45n

unconscious: Blake's in *M*, 117-34;
descent into, in *FZ*, 52-73, 108-
14; in *J*, 159-77, 183; in litera-
ture, 183-86; reactions to, in *FZ*,
51-52, 71-72; in *J*, 155, 159-69,
177-83. *See also* archetype; chaos;
Jung; *prima materia*
Urizen: in *BA*, 19-22; in *BU*,
14-19; in *FZ*, 58, 64-65, 69-70,
85-90, 98-100; in *M*, 125-26,
128, 136-37
uroboros: in *FZ*, 59-61; in *J*,
171-72
Urthona: in *FZ*, 112-15; Spectre of,
70-71

Vala: in *FZ*, 59-61, 99-100, 103-
107; in *J*, 171-73

Yggdrasil, 96

Zoas, *see* Los; Luvah; Tharmas; Uri-
zen; Urthona

Library of Congress Cataloging in Publication Data

Gallant, Christine, 1940-
  Blake and the assimilation of chaos.

  Bibliography: p.
  Includes index.
  1. Blake, William, 1757-1827—Criticism and
interpretation.   2. Myth in literature.   I. Title.
PR4147.G29   821'.7   78-51165
ISBN 0-691-06367-2